PRACTICE MAKES
PERFECT

DENNY VANINGER
WITH DAVE LANGE

PRACTICE MAKES
PERFECT

A GUIDE TO FUN TRAINING SESSIONS FOR 6-10 YEAR OLDS
FROM THE MISSOURI YOUTH SOCCER ASSOCIATION

REEDY PRESS
St. Louis, Missouri

Copyright © 2012, Missouri Youth Soccer Association
All rights reserved.

Reedy Press
PO Box 5131
St. Louis, MO 63139, USA

Library of Congress Control Number: 2012947213

ISBN: 978-1-935806-39-4

For more information, visit www.mysa.org and www.soccermadeinstlouis.com.

Please visit our website at www.reedypress.com.

Design by Jill Halpin   796.334

Printed in the United States of America
12 13 14 15 16   5 4 3 2 1

Contents

Foreword
by Tony Whelan

(Editor's note: Tony Whelan is a distinguished coach and former professional player recognized as one of the most influential people in elite youth soccer. Whelan has been a full-time coach in the youth program of Manchester United, perhaps the world's most recognized sports franchise, since 1998. He also had a long professional playing career in England and the United States. He was a professional at both Manchester United and Manchester City before coming to the United States in 1976. He appeared in 160 games over seven seasons in the North American Soccer League. In 2008, he was voted as one of the 30 most influential black people in English soccer by members of the Football Association, the Professional Footballers Association, and Kick-It-Out, a British anti-racist organization.)

I first encountered Denny Vaninger on Saturday, April 9, 1977, when I was playing for the Fort Lauderdale Strikers versus the St. Louis Stars in the opening game of the North American Soccer League (NASL) season. It was a balmy night as the teams took the field at Lockhart Stadium for the debut of a new franchise in South Florida. Denny was in the prime of his distinguished career, soaring high in the air to open the scoring with a fine header to beat the legendary World Cup–winning goalkeeper Gordon Banks (England, 1966), who was in our goal. We went on to win 2–1, but Denny's performance left an indelible impression on me as he played with so much pride, passion, and commitment for his team. Representing the city of St. Louis (where he was born) clearly meant a great deal to him.

When the season was over, I busied myself working for the Strikers in the community by conducting coaching clinics and generally spreading the gospel of soccer to anyone who would listen. I have to admit that I was a complete novice in this sphere, having been "thrown in at the deep end" and left to fend for myself. I soon realized that I was desperately in need of some help and support, which arrived in a completely unexpected way.

One afternoon, early in 1978, Ron Newman (the Strikers' head coach) informed me that the club had signed Denny on a contract; he asked me to collect Denny from the airport and escort him to the office. I duly obliged, and I recall telling him, excitedly, about the work I was doing in Fort Lauderdale. He listened, intently, and then told me he'd been doing exactly the same thing for quite some time back in St. Louis. It was a "eureka moment" because I instantly knew I had found a kindred spirit who could help me with my coaching program.

The fall of 1978 was a memorable time as we joined forces to try to become the finest ambassadors for soccer and the club as possible in Broward County, Florida. Denny had far more knowledge, experience, and expertise than I had, so I gratefully ate the crumbs from his table for quite some time trying to catch up. Furthermore, he had a wonderfully easy manner with young players, which I greatly admired and strived to emulate. Working alongside him was a major learning curve for me as he taught me so much about player development and coaching methodology. He constantly cajoled and encouraged me to undertake the United States Soccer Federation (USSF) "B" License in January 1979, which was a milestone in my coaching career. I took the "A" course the following year, little knowing that this would eventually lead to my present position at Manchester United. During this time, Denny proved himself to be a mentor *par excellence*, and I owe him a huge debt of gratitude for being such an inspirational role model.

I returned to England in 1983 but continued to keep in touch with him. I also visited St. Louis whenever I could to bask in the warm glow of the Vaninger hospitality, which included as many trips as possible to Ted Drewes for a tub of their amazing ice cream! It has been one of the joys and pleasures of my life to have known him and his family all these years.

I feel profoundly privileged and honored to be invited to write the foreword for this timely and extremely important coaching manual. It is a masterful book written by a master soccer coach and educator. The U6–U10 age group is often deemed by experts to be the "golden age of learning," the optimum period to begin to develop technical excellence and physical literacy. This is the foundation of all long-term player development. It is vital for coaches to understand that incorrect or flawed coaching methods at this stage can seriously hinder a player's progress. More tragically, however, it can actually turn a young player off the sport for life! This is why this book is essential reading for aspiring coaches at this level. The book encapsulates, succinctly, the basic philosophy and principles requisite for coaching very young soccer players, containing a large measure of wisdom and craft knowledge that will be of immense benefit to any coach who reads it and applies its principles in actual practice—namely:

1. To create an environment that is wholly conducive to learning. Make practice fun and the players will learn *for you*—yes, it really is that simple!

2. Understand that player development is not rocket science—it just takes practitioners who really love coaching young people and can inspire them to become better learners.

3. Teaching the "basics" of the game is of paramount importance. Never stop advocating the importance of developing sound technique at a young age.

4. Understand the importance of playing small-sided games. The game is an excellent teacher if we simply allow our players to play without undue interference. In other words, don't over-coach!

5. Realize that children are not "mini adults" and should not be treated as if they are. Childhood is a precious thing, and youngsters should not be deprived of a happy youth by overbearing adults who only want to win soccer matches.

Denny Vaninger is undoubtedly one of the finest soccer coaches of youth players in the USA as well as being a supreme coach educator. I therefore commend his book to you unreservedly, because it is full of sound advice, guidelines, concepts, and strategies that will greatly assist youth coaches within the state of Missouri and beyond whenever they ply their trade.

I have always believed that the most important responsibility for any coach is to instill in young players a love of the game of soccer that will last a lifetime. Therefore, Denny's maxim to make all practice fun will go a long way to ensure that the players will see you as being a "great coach." Great, in the sense that you have inspired your players to want to practice *when you are not there* because they have fallen in love with the game so much. Thus, you have "turned them on" to the joys of simply playing soccer for its own sake, because it really is the beautiful game. Now there's a legacy well worth leaving as you ride off into the sunset.

Tony Whelan
Head of Academy Coaching
Manchester United F.C.
August 14, 2012

Coaching Youth Soccer Players

Youth soccer should be FUN for all players on your team, whether at practice or in games.

As the coach, you make that happen. You are responsible for your players' feelings about how they are doing at practices and in games. You motivate your players by using their names to praise their skills; they will respond by participating eagerly. They will enjoy the entire soccer experience because they realize that you, the coach, are interested in their development as players.

To help them enjoy soccer—and to develop them as players—you must remember two things:

- Soccer is a player's game. There are no timeouts for the coach to send in plays or signal instructions. The players—not the coach—decide what to do in a game and when to do it. How do they learn to play soccer? Simply by playing it, whether in pickup games or at practice. But that doesn't mean you just throw out a ball at practice and let them play. You, the coach, must organize practices that let players develop through activities that are centered on the ball.

- Your practice sessions should be FUN. There is no reason to run laps. Laps have absolutely nothing to do with the sport of soccer. Laps are a waste of time, and they are NOT FUN.

All activities should involve the ball. The more comfortable a player becomes with dribbling, kicking, and passing, the more FUN soccer becomes for the player.

Coaching Philosophy

Youth soccer should be rewarding for everyone, whether they are coaches, players, or parents. The coach makes that happen.

There is more to coaching kids—even very young ones—than just showing up at practice, throwing out a ball, and blowing a whistle. Before that first practice, a coach should develop an approach to teach the game to kids. This approach is called a coaching philosophy.

While each soccer coach has a unique philosophy, those coaches who make soccer rewarding for kids and their parents know "the game" is the best teacher. That is why many youth soccer coaches create a fun environment at practice by playing soccer-related games. Soccer coaches know that the more fun players have, the more effort they will put forth, and therefore the more they will learn about the game. So the key element in a soccer coach's philosophy is an emphasis on making soccer fun.

Young soccer players play on a team to have fun, and to be with their friends. Coaches should make sure that these two things happen at every session, and at every single game. And coaches should have fun, too.

In developing a philosophy to create a fun environment, a coach should decide how to approach three aspects of young players:

- Player development
- Team development
- Personal development

Player development should incorporate your approach to five areas. The first is to use *fun, age-appropriate activities* that focus on the individual player. The second is to encourage *individual creativity* through emphasizing the critical elements of dribbling, speed, and passing. The third is to develop *problem-solving* processes. The fourth is to encourage correct *decision-making* abilities. The fifth and final area is *challenging* the player through competitive training activities.

Team development includes four of the same areas in player development—*fun, age-appropriate activities; problem-solving; decision-making;* and *challenging*—as they apply to your players as a unit. In addition, as part of your coaching philosophy, you must consider how you will approach *skills within the game, systems of play,* and *group cooperation* that develop teamwork.

Personal development covers five areas that are indirectly related to actually playing soccer yet are still important elements of your coaching philosophy. The first covers *team rules* about things such as care of equipment, arrival time before games, and conflicts with other activities. The second is guiding your players to set realistic *personal goals*. The third is your approach to *winning and losing*, and their degree of importance to you. Related to winning/losing is your rationale for allocating *playing time* during games. The final area—and one that is also part of player and team development—is *decision-making*, but here, we mean in the larger sense as a life skill (example: setting priorities correctly, such as school first, soccer second).

Whatever philosophy you develop, make sure that it is appropriate for the age of the players you coach. Very young players new to the game should be coached differently than those who are older, even if by only a few years. For example, a very young player generally has a short attention span and requires simple, action-oriented training exercises rather than complex team drills and coaching lectures. That's why this coaching guide focuses not just on "young players," but on players in three age groups:

- Under-6
- Under-8
- Under-10

You will find exercises, training examples, and practice lesson plans in this coaching guide appropriate to each of these age groups.

Communicating with Parents

Earlier, we wrote that soccer should be rewarding for parents as well as players. While kids play soccer to have fun and be with their friends, parents, first and foremost, look out for their kids. As a result, some parents may want their children to see more playing time or play a different position. Other parents may question your coaching ability. Don't be discouraged. There are ways of communicating with parents in a positive manner that will help make soccer rewarding for them. That's where "team management" comes in. Good team management means keeping parents informed, treating them fairly, and getting them to cooperate.

Two important parts of team management are meeting with parents and involving them with the team.

Parents' meeting

Get the parents together before, or at, the first practice. This may be their first introduction to you, so it's important that you gain their confidence and respect. Getting off on the right foot requires:

- **Appearance**. You don't have to dress like you coach the U.S. National Team. But you don't want to turn off people by looking sloppy. Just follow the rules of good grooming that our moms ingrained in us.

- **Preparation**. Know what you're going to cover beforehand. Set up an agenda in your mind or on handwritten notes, and follow your agenda.

- **Simplicity**. There's no need to deliver the State of the Union address. Tell them what you are going to say. Say it. Then tell them what you said.

- **Handouts**. A sure-fire way to confuse people is to send them home without a handout that covers all the important points, especially your coaching philosophy. Give each person (not just each family) a one-pager with your key messages. Be sure to include the schedule of practices, games, and tournaments; any fees that parents must pay; and any paperwork parents must provide.

- **Dialog**. Encourage questions throughout the meeting. If no one asks, call on someone you already know and ask if he or she has a question. You might even "plant" a question in the audience to get people to open up.

- **Manners**. Start by introducing yourself; ask everyone else to do the same; then thank them for coming. Thank them again at the end.

The content of the meeting should include:

- **Your coaching philosophy**. Make sure that all the parents understand your objectives: to create a fun, educational, and safe environment; to cultivate a love for the game among your players; to ensure that they have fun at practices and games; and to make sure that parents and players enjoy their soccer experience.

- **Your availability to meet with parents**. Say at the meeting, and put in your written handout, that anyone can discuss anything with you after practice.

- **Practice times, duration, and locations**. Hint: Stick to this religiously unless circumstances such as bad weather intervene. Keeping kids for 90 minutes at a practice that was supposed to last an hour will seriously hurt your chances for the "coach of the year" award.

- **Game and tournament schedule**. This should be part of your handout as well as a topic you discuss during the meeting.

- **Fees the parents must pay to cover the team's expenses**. Be sure to itemize the costs so everyone understands where their money is going (for example, league and tournament fees; uniform purchases; practice field rental).

- **Documentation**. Go over all the paperwork (registration, medical forms, copies of birth certificates, etc.) required for kids to play on the team. Make sure everyone understands how to fill out forms and when the completed paperwork is due.

- **Players' responsibilities**. Arrive on time; come prepared to participate; wear proper equipment (shoes, shin guards, etc.); bring water (and ball if you, the coach, decide that you don't want to lug 10 or 20 balls to every practice); dress for the weather; and most importantly, have fun.

- **Parents' responsibilities**. Get kids to practice and games on time; pick up their kids on time; encourage their kids to play fairly; attend games; and respect other kids on the team, their parents, opposing players, coaches and parents, and referees. (It's in the nature of all parents to cheer for their kids, so be sure to cover what's appropriate and what's not.) Most importantly, stress that parents should remember their kids are playing to have fun and to be with their friends.

Lastly, emphasize that the second-to-last parent at the end of practices and games waits until the last parent arrives. This parental responsibility is a good risk management policy. It promotes safety for the kids by ensuring that the coach is always with a minimum of two other adults after games and practices.

One question that usually comes up at the first meeting is: "How can I help?" You, being the prepared coach, will come to the meeting with answers ready that cover:

Parent participation

One way to get the parents on board is to provide opportunities for them to help. Some of the traditional parental roles include:

- **Team manager**, who is the liaison between the coach and the rest of the parents. The coach can delegate any number of responsibilities to the manager, such as distributing, collecting, and submitting player forms; handling finances (uniform purchases, player fees, league and tournament entry fees); reserving hotel rooms for out-of-town tournaments; and organizing team events such as parties, picnics, and fund-raisers.

- **Phone/e-mail coordinator**, who maintains the system used to contact parents with urgent announcements such as rainouts, location changes, and tournament pairings.

- **Refreshment coordinator**, who is responsible for treating the kids to orange slices at halftime and snacks after the game. (Kids usually don't remember the scores, but they always will remember those halftime oranges!)

- **"New media" coordinator**, a job for any parents who fancy themselves as electronic gurus with ambitions to video the games, set up a team website, or maintain a team account on Facebook and/or Twitter. Make sure that this person follows legal procedures regarding privacy as it pertains to posting images and information (especially regarding minors) on-line.

There are many other ways to enlist the help of parents. The more involved they become in constructive support, the better. And the easier it is for the coach, who (theoretically, at least) will have less to worry about.

Participation:
Keeping Players Involved, Motivated, and Having Fun

Coaches should know and understand why players come to practice, go to games, and travel to tournaments. They don't choose to do those things. Their parents sign up the kids and bring them. Learning to play soccer is not why kids practice, play, and travel. Kids do them to have fun and to be with their friends.

A typical story involves a team of U-10 players who traveled to a tournament 200 miles from home. When the team arrived at the hotel, three players ran up to the front desk and asked the manager, "Where is the swimming pool?"

The manager said, "We do not have a swimming pool."

The players immediately ran to the coach and parents and said: "We must be at the wrong hotel. They don't have a swimming pool."

The coach said, "We're here to play soccer, not swim."

The players were very disappointed. The young players were at the hotel to have fun and swim. Soccer games were going to get in their way of having fun at the pool!

This little story shows how a coach can turn soccer into a chore that kids dread rather than a game they love to play. Coaches should focus on fun for the players all of the time. Traveling, practices, games—anything involving the kids—should be fun!

The challenge for you, the coach, is to teach kids to play soccer through fun activities that keep them involved, motivated, and having fun.

Activities to involve players

Every practice should include a ball for each player. The more players touch the ball, the more comfortable and confident they will become. Movements such as running, jumping, and skipping are fun, especially using a soccer ball.

Be prepared: Have many activities planned for your practice sessions.

Make sure to find moments at each practice to praise each player by name. Players will participate at their individual highest levels when the coach tells them by name that they are doing something well:

"Way to dribble, Meghan."

"Wow, Kevin, you are a fast runner."

"Jeffrey, you are a good soccer player."

Positive reinforcement encourages players and makes them feel special at practice.

Last, but not least: Enjoy practice as much as you want your players to enjoy it.

Remember, you will create lasting soccer memories for your players . . .

- Scoring their first goals
- Fun at practices and games
- Parents and relatives watching the games
- The excitement of playing in a game
- Getting that first pair of shin guards and putting them on without help
- Playing soccer with friends
- The smell in the air at soccer practices
- Oranges at halftimes
- Getting their first soccer uniforms
- Being on a soccer team
- Remembering their soccer coaches
- Playing with their friends after games
- Traveling to soccer tournaments
- Team parties and sleep-overs
- Getting a medal or a trophy

U-6

Kids under the age of 6 are full of energy. They are beginning to learn to read and write. There are minimal differences between boys and girls. But U-6 players cannot understand more complex concepts such as working together. These are some of the key characteristics that coaches must remember to create a fun and educational experience for U-6 players.

Coaches of U-6 players should:

- Keep everything simple. Kids at this age have very short attention spans. Activities should have few rules.

- Channel their energy into games that include running, jumping, rolling on the ground, and retrieving balls.

- Focus on individuality by having a ball for each player. Don't expect them to play collectively, even though they may verbalize team concepts.

- Let them play without pressure.

- Praise them frequently by name. Kids at this age are sensitive and self-centered. They enjoy showing off. ("Watch me," they say often.) They love to hear that they are doing something well.

- Tap into their passion to imagine and pretend. For example, instead of telling them to "dribble from this cone to that cone over there," give the cones the names of cartoon characters the kids love or towns where the kids live.

These traits of U-6 players are incorporated into the following lesson plans and exercises.

Lesson plans for U-6 players – Lesson plan No. 1

Exercises	Description	Activity focus	Minutes
Activity 1 Warmup: Body part dribble	1. Roll the ball forward, backward, and sideways with left and right elbow. 2. Roll the ball forward, backward, and sideways with right and left hands. 3. Coach calls out body part, player uses that body part to touch the ball. 4. Introduce "in-between" (pass the ball from inside of right foot to inside of left foot) 5. Keep track of time for each segment (15 seconds, etc.)	• Improve dribbling • Awareness of player on field • Change speed of dribbling • Soccer-related activity	10
Activity 2 Cone maze	1. Distribute cones/markers randomly in area approximately 20x20 yards. 2. Players dribble around cones indiscriminately. 3. Players dribble around one cone and back to home base cone. 4. Change exercise by using only one foot; sole of foot; outside of feet; both feet; toe touches at the cone; in-betweens at cone. 5. Players can score goals by dribbling through any two cones; how many goals can players score in 30 seconds?	• Vision of field • Dribbling skills • Use of both feet • Dribbling to cone and back to base • Peripheral vision (knowledge of where players are on field)	10

20 Yards

20 Yards

Activity 3
Scoring goals

1. Set up field with two goals.
2. Coach stands at midfield.
3. Coach directs players to dribble and score goal, leave ball there, and run back to coach.
4. Coach moves to different area of field, tells players to retrieve ball, run back to coach, dribble and score, leave ball, and run back to coach.
5. Coach moves again and continues exercise.

- Scoring goals
- Avoiding other players on field
- Peripheral vision (knowledge of where players are on field)
- Dribbling
- Kicking into goals
- Goal-scoring, not shooting

10

Activity 4
Red light, green light

1. Each player has a ball.
2. Coach stands 10 yards from players.
3. Coach says, "Green light." All players dribble to coach.
4. Coach says, "Red light." All players stop ball by putting one foot on top of ball.
5. Coach changes positions, repeats drill by saying red light or green light.

- Dribbling
- Running with ball
- Avoiding other players with balls
- Coach represents the goal

10

15 Yards

20 Yards

Play the game:
3 players vs. 3 players

1. Set up field with goals about 20 yards apart.
2. Play 3 players vs. 3 players.
3. No limitations.
4. No goalkeepers.

- Find the goal
- Dribbling past defenders
- Having FUN playing the game
- Learning which direction to run
- Scoring goals

15-20

20 Yards

20 Yards

Lesson plans for U-6 players – Lesson plan No. 2

Exercises	Description	Activity focus	Minutes
Activity 1 Warmup: I can do this	1. Coach holds ball above head. "I can do this, can you?" Players follow coach's lead. 2. Players suggest other things (toe touches, throwing ball up in air and catching it, dribbling moves, and so forth).	• Having FUN • General warm-up • Ball skills • Players in charge of activity	10
Activity 2 Scoring goals	1. Set up field with two goals. 2. Coach stands at midfield. 3. Coach directs players to dribble and score goal, leave ball there, and run back to coach. 4. Coach moves to different area of field, tells players to retrieve ball, run back to coach, dribble and score, leave ball, and run back to coach. 5. Coach moves again and continues exercise.	• Scoring goals • Avoiding other players on field • Peripheral vision (knowledge of where players are on field) • Dribbling • Kicking into goals • Goal-scoring, not shooting	10

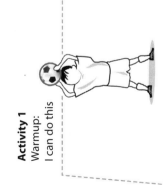

Activity 3
Ball retrieve

1. Each player has a ball.

2. Players gather around coach and hand soccer balls to coach.

3. Coach randomly tosses balls; players return using coach's instruction (dribble with right foot only, dribble with left foot only, and so forth).

- Peripheral vision (knowledge of where players and coach are on field)   10
- Coach represents the goal
- Dribbling with different parts of feet while running with the ball

Activity 4
Juggling

1. Each player holds a ball.

2. Player drops ball and tries to kick the ball back to hands. Try to use thighs and feet to keep ball in the air.

3. Player holds ball with both hands and kicks with shoe laces, not releasing the ball.

4. Have the players count how many times they touch the ball without it touching the ground.

- Eye and body coordination   10
- Feeling comfortable with the ball
- Individual competition (number of juggles)
- Having FUN with the ball

Play the game:
3 players vs. 3 players

1. Set up field with goals about 20 yards apart.

2. Play 3 players vs. 3 players.

3. No limitations.

4. No goalkeepers.

- Find the goal   15–20
- Dribbling past defenders
- Having FUN playing the game
- Learning which direction to run
- Scoring goals

20 Yards

20 Yards

Lesson plans for U-6 players - Lesson plan No. 3

Exercises	Description	Activity focus	Minutes
Activity 1 Warmup: Dribbling on "go"	1. Create circle with cones/markers 15 yards across. 2. Each player has a ball and stands by a cone/marker. 3. When coach says "Go," players dribble across the circle and back to original cone. 4. Other variations on word "go": • Players dribble to nearest cone. • Players dribble with one foot across circle and back. • Players dribble with soles of feet only across circle and back. • Players dribble with outside of feet only across circle and back.	• Dribbling • Running with ball • Awareness of other players • Dribbling moves	10
Activity 2 Duck duck goose	1. Players sit in circle, each player with a ball. 2. One player stands and dribbles around circle, touches everyone's head saying "duck duck." 3. When player says "goose," the "goose" must chase player back to original spot. 4. Continue until every player gets to be the chaser.	• Having FUN • Dribbling • Dribbling while running • Dribbling with control and speed	10

Activity 3
Rest area

1. Each player has ball.

2. Coach says, "everybody rest." Players do whatever they want with their feet on the ball:

   • Put one foot on ball.

   • Pull ball back with bottom of foot.

   • Dribble around another player.

   • Standing and keep ball moving with both feet.

10

• Catching players' breath

• Resting before next activity

• Ball touches

• Getting comfortable with ball

Activity 4
Scoring goals

1. Set up field with two goals.

2. Coach stands at midfield.

3. Coach directs players to dribble and score goal, leave ball there, and run back to coach.

4. Coach moves to different area of field, tells players to retrieve ball, run back to coach, dribble and score, leave ball, and run back to coach.

5. Coach moves again and continues exercise.

10

• Scoring goals

• Avoiding other players on field

• Peripheral vision (knowledge of where players are on field)

• Dribbling

• Kicking into goals

• Goal-scoring, not shooting

Play the game:
3 players vs. 3 players

1. Set up field with goals about 20 yards apart.

2. Play 3 players vs. 3 players.

3. No limitations.

4. No goalkeepers.

15-20

• Find the goal

• Dribbling past defenders

• Having FUN playing the game

• Learning which direction to run

• Scoring goals

20 Yards

20 Yards

Lesson plans for U-6 players - Lesson plan No. 4

Exercises	Description	Activity focus	Minutes
Activity 1 Warmup: Ball retrieve	1. Each player has a ball. 2. Players gather around coach and hand soccer balls to coach. 3. Coach randomly tosses balls; players return using coach's instruction (dribble with right foot only, dribble with left foot only, and so forth).	• Peripheral vision (knowledge of where players and coach are on field) • Coach represents the goal • Dribbling with different parts of feet while running with the ball	10
Activity 2 Dribbling on "go"	1. Create circle with cones/markers 15 yards across. 2. Each player has a ball and stands by a cone/marker. 3. When coach says "Go," players dribble across the circle and back to original cone. 4. Other variations on word "go": • Players dribble to nearest cone. • Players dribble with one foot across circle and back. • Players dribble with soles of feet only across circle and back. • Players dribble with outside of feet only across circle and back.	• Dribbling • Running with ball • Awareness of other players • Dribbling moves	10

Activity 3
Numbers game

1. Set up field with goals about 20 yards apart.
2. Place ball at midfield.
3. Group players into two teams, have players count off, and tell them to remember their numbers.
4. Coach calls out a number. The player with that number from each team runs to the ball. First player to reach the ball tries to score and the second player defends until a goal is scored or the ball goes out of bounds.
5. Coach throws out another ball and calls different number.
   - Start with 1 vs. 1
   - Progress to 2 vs. 2
   - Progress to 3 vs. 3

- Defending   10
- Dribbling
- Scoring
- Field awareness
- Having FUN by playing soccer

Activity 4
Grab soccer balls

1. Set up square 20x20 yards.
2. Group players into two equal teams.
3. One team is positioned in one corner of the field; the other team in the diagonally opposite corner.
4. Put all balls at midfield.
5. Coach says "Go"; both teams try to retrieve as many balls as possible from middle of field and dribble them to their areas.
6. Once all balls are collected, players can "steal" balls from the other team's area.
7. Continue for 60 seconds and repeat

- Dribbling   10
- Shielding
- Running with the ball
- Knowing where the ball is
- Defending

Play the game:
3 players vs. 3 players

1. Set up field with goals about 20 yards apart.
2. Play 3 players vs. 3 players.
3. No limitations.
4. No goalkeepers.

- Find the goal   15-20
- Dribbling past defenders
- Having FUN playing the game
- Learning which direction to run
- Scoring goals

Lesson plans for U-6 players - Lesson plan No. 5

Exercises	Description	Activity focus	Minutes

Activity 1
Warmup: Ball exercises
	1. Each player has a ball.
	2. Players run, throw balls in the air, and catch them.
	3. Players skip, throw balls in the air, and catch them.
	4. Players run backward, throw balls in the air, and catch them.
	5. Players juggle balls:
	  • Both feet
	  • Right foot only
	  • Left foot only
	  • Heading only
	6. Players sit:
	  • Hold ball in hands, touch with instep of foot, alternating right and left
	  • Use feet to juggle ball
	  • Squeeze ball with inside of both feet and lift the ball
		• Having FUN
		• Running
		• Dribbling
		• General warmup
			10

Activity 2
Follow the leader
	1. Each player has a ball.
	2. Coach designates one player as the leader.
	3. Leader runs around field doing anything he/she wants, and the rest of the players follow the leader. Examples:
	  • Dribbling
	  • Holding ball in air
	  • Holding ball while skipping
	4. Repeat until each player has a turn as the leader.
		• Having FUN
		• Dribbling
		• Following direction of leader
			10

Activity 3
1 player vs. 1 player

1. Set up several fields 20x15 yards.
2. One ball per field.
3. One player plays against other player for 90 seconds and tries to score as many goals as possible.
4. When goal is scored or ball goes out of bounds, coach serves another ball to attacking player.
5. Players switch roles.
6. Rotate opponents until each player has played against every player on field.

- Shielding
- Dribbling
- Scoring
- Transition (offense to defense)
- Having FUN playing soccer

10

Activity 4
Scoring goals

1. Set up field with two goals.
2. Coach stands at midfield.
3. Coach directs players to dribble and score goal, leave ball there, and run back to coach.
4. Coach moves to different area of field, tells players to retrieve ball, run back to coach, dribble and score, leave ball, and run back to coach.
5. Coach moves again and continues exercise.

- Scoring goals
- Avoiding other players on field
- Peripheral vision (knowledge of where players are on field)
- Dribbling
- Kicking into goals
- Goal-scoring, not shooting

10

Play the game:
3 players vs. 3 players

1. Set up field with goals about 20 yards apart.
2. Play 3 players vs. 3 players.
3. No limitations.
4. No goalkeepers.

- Find the goal
- Dribbling past defenders
- Having FUN playing the game
- Learning which direction to run
- Scoring goals

15-20

Lesson plans for U-6 players - Lesson plan No. 6

Exercises	Description	Activity focus	Minutes
Activity 1 Warmup: Everybody is "it" 	1. Set up square 20x20 yards. 2. Each player has a ball. 3. Players dribble inside area, tagging as many other players as they can. (Each player is "it.") 4. Change game by only tagging person with right or left hand; tagging person on shoulder; tagging person on knee.	• Having FUN • Awareness of other players on field • Dribbling • Avoiding other players	10
Activity 2 Cone maze 	1. Distribute cones/markers randomly in area approximately 20x20 yards. 2. Players dribble around cones indiscriminately. 3. Players dribble around one cone and back to home base cone. 4. Change exercise by using only one foot; sole of foot; outside of feet, both feet; toe touches at the cone; in-betweens at cone. 5. Players can score goals by dribbling through any two cones; how many goals can players score in 30 seconds?	• Vision of field • Dribbling skills • Use of both feet • Dribbling to cone and back to base • Peripheral vision (knowledge of where players are on field)	10

Activity 3
Relay races

10

1. Set up two lines of cones, one "home" line 20 yards from the "away" line.
2. Group players into even teams, each team with one ball lined up behind a cone on the "home" line.
3. On coach's command, first player in each line goes to away cone and back; next player in line goes when the first player reaches the "home" cone.
4. First team to have all players return "home" wins.
5. Variations include:
   • Sprinting   • Dribbling
   • Dribbling to "away" cone, passing to teammate at "home" cone

• Dribbling
• Passing
• Having FUN

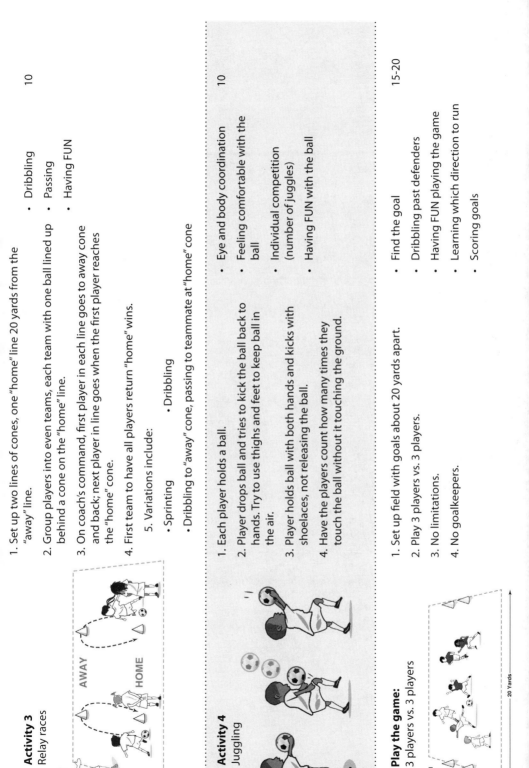

Activity 4
Juggling

10

1. Each player holds a ball.
2. Player drops ball and tries to kick the ball back to hands. Try to use thighs and feet to keep ball in the air.
3. Player holds ball with both hands and kicks with shoelaces, not releasing the ball.
4. Have the players count how many times they touch the ball without it touching the ground.

• Eye and body coordination
• Feeling comfortable with the ball
• Individual competition (number of juggles)
• Having FUN with the ball

Play the game:
3 players vs. 3 players

15-20

1. Set up field with goals about 20 yards apart.
2. Play 3 players vs. 3 players.
3. No limitations.
4. No goalkeepers.

• Find the goal
• Dribbling past defenders
• Having FUN playing the game
• Learning which direction to run
• Scoring goals

20 Yards

20 Yards

Lesson plans for U-6 players - Lesson plan No. 7

Exercises	Description	Activity focus	Minutes
Activity 1 Warmup: Scoring goals	1. Set up field with two goals. 2. Coach stands at midfield. 3. Coach directs players to dribble and score goal, leave ball there, and run back to coach. 4. Coach moves to different area of field, tells players to retrieve ball, run back to coach, dribble and score, leave ball, and run back to coach. 5. Coach moves again and continues exercise.	• Scoring goals • Avoiding other players on field • Peripheral vision (knowledge of where players are on field) • Dribbling • Kicking into goals • Goal-scoring, not shooting	10
Activity 2 Everybody is "it"	1. Set up square 20x20 yards. 2. Each player has a ball. 3. Players dribble inside area, tagging as many other players as they can. (Each player is "it.") 4. Change game by only tagging person with right or left hand; tagging person on shoulder; tagging person on knee.	• Having FUN • Awareness of other players on field • Dribbling • Avoiding other players	10

20 Yards

20 Yards

Activity 3
Where is the coach?

1. Each player has a ball.

2. Players close eyes and coach moves.

3. Coach says, "Where's coach?" Players open eyes and dribble to coach.

4. Progress to where coach is moving after players open their eyes.

- Find the goal (coach)
- Dribble in one direction
- Dribble using both feet, one foot, etc.
- Avoiding defenders
- Having FUN

10

Activity 4
Ball retrieve

1. Each player has a ball.

2. Players gather around coach and hand soccer balls to coach.

3. Coach randomly tosses balls; players return using coach's instruction (dribble with right or left foot only; dribble with inside or outside of foot only; and so forth)

- Peripheral vision (knowledge of where players and coach are on field)
- Coach represents the goal
- Dribbling with different parts of feet while running with the ball

10

Play the game:
3 players vs. 3 players

1. Set up field with goals about 20 yards apart.

2. Play 3 players vs. 3 players.

3. No limitations.

4. No goalkeepers.

- Find the goal
- Dribbling past defenders
- Having FUN playing the game
- Learning which direction to run
- Scoring goals

15-20

20 Yards

20 Yards

Lesson plans for U-6 players - Lesson plan No. 8

Exercises	Description	Activity focus	Minutes
Activity 1 Warmup: Fun dribbling 	1. Each player has a ball. 2. All players dribbling using different parts of feet (shoelaces, soles, inside of feet, outside of feet) 3. Progression: • Change speed • Change direction • Use dribbling moves	• Dribbling • Changing speed • Using different parts of feet (soles, inside, outside)	10
Activity 2 Moving goals 	1. Group players into two equal teams. 2. Each team has a ball. 3. Two coaches or parents stretch a practice vest or rope between them to make a goal. 4. Each team tries to score through either side of the goal as the goal moves around.	• Scoring • Dribbling • Passing • Awareness (keeping head up to see the goal)	10

Activity 3
Tail tag

1. Each player tucks a practice vest into the back of the shorts.

2. Players try to take vests from other players.

3. Last player with vest tucked into shorts wins.

4. Progression: Each player dribbles a ball while trying to take vests.

- Awareness of other players on field
- Dribbling with heads up
- Having FUN

10

Activity 4
1 player vs. 1 player

1. Set up several fields 20x15 yards wide.

2. One ball per field.

3. One player plays against other player for 90 seconds and tries to score as many goals as possible.

4. When goal is scored or ball goes out of bounds, coach serves another ball to attacking player.

5. Players switch roles.

6. Rotate opponents until each player has played against every player on field.

- Shielding
- Dribbling
- Scoring
- Transition (offense to defense)
- Having FUN (playing soccer)

10

Play the game:
3 players vs. 3 players

1. Set up field with goals about 20 yards apart.

2. Play 3 players vs. 3 players.

3. No limitations.

4. No goalkeepers.

- Find the goal
- Dribbling past defenders
- Having FUN playing the game
- Learning which direction to run
- Scoring goals

15-20

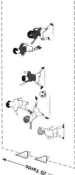

Lesson plans for U-6 players - Lesson plan No. 9

Exercises

Activity 1
Warmup: Ball retrieve

Activity 2
Relay races

Description

1. Each player has a ball.

2. Players gather around coach and hand soccer balls to coach.

3. Coach randomly tosses balls; players return using coach's instruction (dribble with right or left foot only; inside or outside of foot only; and so forth).

1. Set up two lines of cones, one "home" line 20 yards from the "away" line.

2. Group players into even teams, each team with one ball lined up behind a cone on the "home" line.

3. On coach's command, first player in each line goes to away cone and back; next player in line goes when the first player reaches the "home" cone.

4. First team to have all players return "home" wins.

5. Variations include:
   • Sprinting   • Dribbling
   • Dribbling to "away" cone, passing to teammate at "home" cone

Activity focus

• Peripheral vision (knowledge of where players and coach are on field)

• Coach represents the goal

• Dribbling with different parts of feet while running with the ball

• Dribbling
• Passing
• Having FUN

Minutes

10

10

Activity 3
Rest area

1. Each player has ball.

2. Coach says, "everybody rest." Players do whatever they want with their feet on the ball:
   - Put one foot on ball.
   - Pull ball back with bottom of foot.
   - Dribble around another player.
   - Standing and keep ball moving with both feet.

10

- Catching players' breath
- Resting before next activity
- Ball touches
- Getting comfortable with ball

Activity 4
Scoring goals

1. Set up field with two goals.

2. Coach stands at midfield.

3. Coach directs players to dribble and score goal, leave ball there, and run back to coach.

4. Coach moves to different area of field, tells players to retrieve ball, run back to coach, dribble and score, leave ball, and run back to coach.

5. Coach moves again and continues exercise.

10

- Scoring goals
- Avoiding other players on field
- Peripheral vision (knowledge of where players are on field)
- Dribbling
- Kicking into goals
- Goal-scoring, not shooting

Play the game:
3 players vs. 3 players

1. Set up field with goals about 20 yards apart.

2. Play 3 players vs. 3 players.

3. No limitations.

4. No goalkeepers.

15-20

- Find the goal
- Dribbling past defenders
- Having FUN playing the game
- Learning which direction to run
- Scoring goals

20 Yards

20 yards

Lesson plans for U-6 players - Lesson plan No. 10

Exercises	Description	Activity focus	Minutes
Activity 1 Warmup: Ba l skills 	1. Each player has a ball. 2. Use hands to move ball in a figure 8 around legs. 3. Use hands to move ball around waist. 4. Throw and catch. 5. Bounce off thigh and catch. 6. Tap top or side of ball with feet; see how many taps a player can do in 10 seconds. 7. Use balls of feet to roll ball around. 8. Jump back and forth over the ball.	• Ball control • Eye and body coordination	10
Activity 2 Tail tag 	1. Each player tucks a practice vest into the back of the shorts. 2. Players try to take vests from other players. 3. Last player with vest tucked into shorts wins. 4. Progression: Each player dribbles a ball while trying to take vests.	• Awareness of other players on field • Dribbling with heads up • Having FUN	10

Activity 3
Juggling

1. Each player holds a ball.

2. Player drops ball and tries to kick the ball back to hands. Try to use thighs and feet to keep ball in the air.

3. Player holds ball with both hands and kicks with shoelaces, not releasing the ball.

4. Have the players count how many times they touch the ball without it touching the ground.

- Eye and body coordination   10
- Feeling comfortable with the ball
- Individual competition (number of juggles)
- Having FUN with the ball

Activity 4
Cone maze

20 Yards

20 Yards

1. Distribute cones/markers randomly in area approximately 20x20 yards.

2. Players dribble around cones indiscriminately.

3. Players dribble around one cone and back to home base cone.

4. Change exercise by using only one foot; sole of foot; outside of feet, both feet; toe touches at the cone; in-betweens at cone.

5. Players can score goals by dribbling through any two cones; how many goals can players score in 30 seconds?

- Vision of field   10
- Dribbling skills
- Use of both feet
- Dribbling to cone and back to base
- Peripheral vision (knowledge of where players are on field)

Play the game:
3 players vs. 3 players

20 Yards

20 Yards

1. Set up field with goals about 20 yards apart.

2. Play 3 players vs. 3 players.

3. No limitations.

4. No goalkeepers.

- Find the goal   15-20
- Dribbling past defenders
- Having FUN playing the game
- Learning which direction to run
- Scoring goals

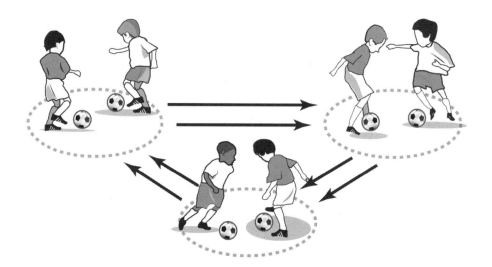

Exercise No. 1: Three-circle dribble

1. Set up three circles 5 yards in diameter in an area 20x20 yards.
2. Divide into three teams, one team per circle.
3. On coach's command, players dribble to another circle.
4. Rest in circle, touching ball for 30-40 seconds while standing.

Variations:

- Dribble from your home circle around another circle and back to home circle.
- Dribble around two circles and back to home.
- Dribble using right or left foot only.
- Dribble using inside or outside of foot only.
- Dribble using soles of feet only.

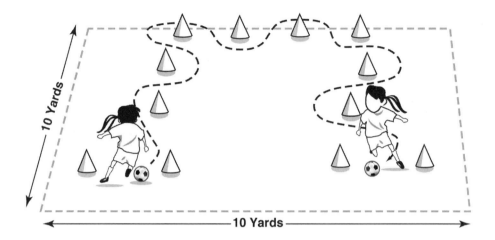

Exercise No. 2: Dribbling

1. Set up a square 10x10 yards with cones lining three sides of square.

2. Each player has a ball and all players line up behind the "home" cones.

3. On coach's command, first player dribbles around cones and through "goal" cones.

4. Another player follows every few seconds.

Variations:

  • Right or left foot only.

  • Inside or outside of feet only.

  • Increase speed.

  • Have players start at "goal" cones and dribble around cones back to "home" cones.

Exercise No. 3: Bunch of soccer balls

1. Play on a normal-size field for 6-year-olds with goals.

2. Play 3 players vs. 3 players.

3. No goalkeepers.

4. Start game with more than one ball. (Using two, three, or four balls creates opportunities for 1 vs. 1 or 1 vs. 0 and dribbling activities suitable for 6-year-olds.)

5. Coach takes out one ball at a time until one ball is left.

Exercise No. 4: Knee tag

1. Set up grid 10x15 yards.

2. Each player has a ball.

3. Players dribble and collect a point each time they tag another player on the knee.

4. Player with most points at end of the game (about 60-90 seconds) wins.

Variations:

- Dribble with right or left foot only.

- Use inside of feet only.

- Tag right knee or left knee only.

Exercise No. 5: **Team dribbling**

1. Set up grid 20x20 yards.

2. Group players into two equal teams.

3. Each player on one team has a ball; other team does not have any.

4. On coach's command, team with balls dribbles and tries to keep possession while other team tries to take them away.

5. Team with most balls at end of the game (about 60-90 seconds) wins.

6. Repeat with other team starting with balls.

Exercise No. 6: Crab soccer

1. Set up grid 20x15 yards wide.

2. Two players get in crawling position in the middle of the grid and are "crabs."

3. Each of the remaining players has a ball and starts at one end of the grid.

4. On coach's command, players try to dribble to other end without a "crab" kicking the ball out of the field.

5. Each player who loses a ball becomes a "crab."

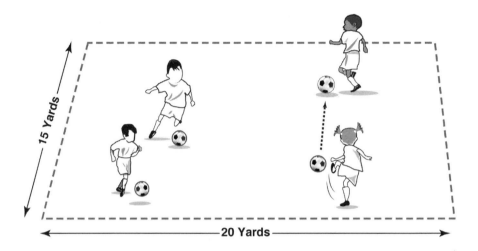

Exercise No. 7: Ball tag

1. Set up grid 20x15 yards wide.

2. Each player has a ball.

3. On coach's command, players begin dribbling and try to hit another player's feet or ball with their ball.

4. A player gets a point for hitting another player's ball or feet with the ball.

5. Player with most points at end of the game (60-90 seconds) wins.

Variations:

- Right foot or left foot only.
- Inside or outside of foot only.

Exercise No. 8: Dribble and stop

1. Each player has a ball.

2. Players dribble.

3. On coach's command, players stop, then start at full speed.

4. Coach repeats command at irregular intervals.

Variations:

- Right foot or left foot only.

- Inside or outside of foot only.

- Change directions.

Exercise No. 9: Animal game

1. Each player has a ball.

2. Players dribble.

3. Coach calls out the name of an animal, and players have to act like that animal while dribbling.

Variations:

- Right foot or left foot only.
- Inside or outside of foot only.

Exercise No. 10: Dribbling with speed

1.   Each player has a ball.

2.   Players dribble 5-10 yards as fast as they can, pick up the balls, and kick them as high as they can.

3.   Repeat for about a minute.

Variations:

- Dribble with right foot or left foot only.
- Dribble with inside or outside of foot only.
- Throw with one or two hands.
- Kick with right or left foot only.

U-8

Kids in the U-8 age group are developing rapidly physically and mentally. Some characteristics have changed little since U-6. U-8 players still have lots of energy, they love to pretend, and there are minimal differences between boys and girls. But U-8 players have much better coordination, their attention span is longer, their vocabulary is much larger, and they are beginning to understand time and space. Coaches of U-8 players create a fun and educational atmosphere that focuses on these unique characteristics.

Coaches of U-8 players should:

- Introduce combinations with partners. U-8 kids enjoy playing in pairs.

- Praise individual players for trying hard, even if they struggle. Kids in this age group equate effort with success, are sensitive to criticism, and dislike failure in front of others.

- Stress kicking and dribbling exercises that allow players to use their newly found coordination.

- Turn exercises at practice into games such as dribbling races, shooting contests, and juggling competitions. U-8 players like to play competitive games.

These traits of U-8 players are incorporated into the following lesson plans and exercises.

Lesson plans for U-8 players - Lesson plan No. 1

Exercises	Description	Activity focus	Minutes
Activity 1 Warmup: Ball retrieve with a partner	1. Players pair off, one ball per pair. 2. Each pair gives ball to coach, who throws ball. 3. Each pair brings ball back by passing ball to each other using inside or outside of feet, touching the ball 20 times, etc.	• Passing • Dribbling • Field awareness • Going to goal (the coach)	10
Activity 2 Follow your partner	1. Players pair off, one ball per pair. 2. One player leads by dribbling the ball in an area 20x20 yards; the other player follows. 3. Switch roles after one minute.	• Keeping ball close to the body • Changing direction • Dribbling using different parts of each foot	10

Activity 3
Goal-scoring partners

10

1. Set up multiple goals, each goal consisting of two cones 2 yards apart, in an area 25x25 yards.
2. Pair off, one ball per pair.
3. Score as many goals as possible by passing ball through goal to partner.
4. Keep track of how many goals are scored.
5. Repeat and try to score more goals than in last attempt.
6. Progression: left foot only, right foot only, inside of foot only, etc.

• Scoring goals
• Changing directions
• Passing with partner
• Decision-making
• Teamwork

Activity 4
Passing

10

1. Pair off, one ball per pair.
2. Pass ball back and forth between two cones 6 yards apart.
3. Ball must stay on ground and go through cones without touching them.
4. Progression: one, two, or three touches per pass; or one touch using different parts of foot

• Passing
• Concentrating on ball
• Scoring goals
• Working with teammate

Play the game:
4 players vs. 4 players

15-20

1. Set up field with goals about 30 yards apart.
2. Play 4 players vs. 4 players.
3. No limitations.
4. No goalkeepers.

• Making decisions
• Solving problems
• Dribbling
• Passing
• Having FUN playing the game
• Teamwork
• Scoring goals

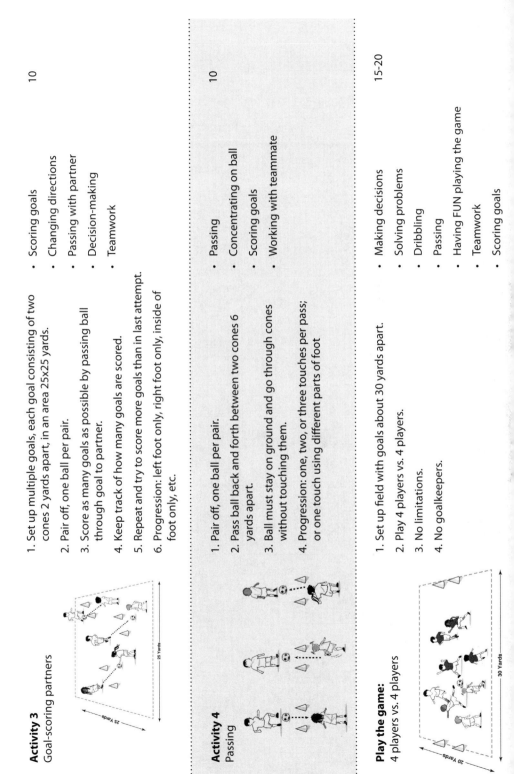

Lesson plans for U-8 players – Lesson plan No. 2

Exercises	Description	Activity focus	Minutes
Activity 1 Warmup: Juggling	1. Each player holds a ball. 2. Player drops ball and tries to kick the ball back to hands. Try to use thighs and feet to keep ball in the air. 3. Have the players count how many times they touch the ball without it touching the ground.	• Eye and body coordination • Feeling comfortable with the ball • Individual competition (number of juggles) • Having FUN with the ball	10
Activity 2 Everybody is "it"	1. Set up square 20x20 yards. 2. Each player has a ball. 3. Players dribble inside area, tagging as many other players as they can. (Each player is "it.") 4. Progression: Tag person with right or left hand; tag person on shoulder; tag person on knee.	• Having FUN • Awareness of other players on field • Dribbling • Avoiding other players	10

20 Yards

20 Yards

Activity 3
Freeze tag

1. Set up square 25x25 yards.

2. All players except one have a ball. Player without ball is "it."

3. Person who is "it" tags a player dribbling with a ball. That player holds ball over head, spreads legs and is "frozen."

4. Player is "unfrozen" when a ball is dribbled between the player's legs.

5. Change person who is "it" every 45-60 seconds.

15

- Dribbling
- Shielding
- Peripheral vision
- Awareness of defender
- Scoring goals
- Making decisions

25 Yards

Activity 4
Passing with a partner

1. Players pair off, one ball per pair.

2. Players pass ball back and forth to partners while running.

3. Progression: Limit to one, two, or three touches.

10

- Passing
- Dribbling
- Vision of field
- Communicating with partner
- Running into open space

Play the game:
2 players vs. 2 players

1. Set up square 25x25 yards with goals 12 feet wide at each end.

2. Play 2 players vs. 2 players.

3. Players score by passing through goal, dribbling through goal, or stopping ball on goal line.

15-20

- Dribbling
- Passing
- Receiving
- Defending
- Having FUN playing the game
- Communicating
- Scoring goals

25 Yards

Lesson plans for U-8 players - Lesson plan No. 3

Exercises	Description	Activity focus	Minutes
Activity 1 Warmup: Dribbling moves 25 YARDS	1. Set up circle 25 yards across. 2. Each player has a ball. 3. Pick a player to demonstrate a dribbling move. 4. All players do dribbling move for one minute. 5. Pick another player to demonstrate another dribbling move.	• Dribbling • Field awareness • Making decisions	10
Activity 2 Players act as coach 	1. Players pair off, one ball per pair. 2. Player without the ball is the "coach." 3. "Coach" commands player what to do: dribbling; passing through coach's legs; retrieving the ball; etc. 4. Change coaches after one minute.	• Dribbling • Following directions • Field awareness	10

Activity 3
1 player vs. 1 player

20 Yards

1. Divide players into groups of four.

2. Two players 20 yards apart are goal posts; two players in middle play 1 player vs. 1 player.

3. Player scores by hitting the "goal post" with the ball or dribbling past the "goal post."

4. Play one minute and rotate: Goal posts become players; players become goal posts.

5. Rotate players to other groups.

15

- Transition
- Attacking
- Defending
- Goal-scoring
- Shielding
- Tackling
- Having FUN playing the game

Activity 4
Juggling with partner

1. Players pair off, one ball per pair.

2. Pass ball back and forth using feet or thighs without ball touching the ground.

3. Count how many times the players touch the ball before it hits the ground.

10

- Eye-foot coordination
- Communicating
- Making decisions
- Getting comfortable with the ball

Play the game:
4 players vs. 4 players

30 Yards

20 Yards

1. Set up field with goals about 30 yards apart.

2. Play 4 players vs. 4 players.

3. No limitations.

4. No goalkeepers.

15-20

- Making decisions
- Solving problems
- Dribbling
- Passing
- Having FUN playing the game
- Teamwork
- Scoring goals

Lesson plans for U-8 players - Lesson plan No. 4

Exercises	Description	Activity focus	Minutes
Activity 1 Warmup: Possession with partner	1. Set up square 25x25 yards. 2. Players pair off, one ball per pair. 3. One player starts with the ball. 4. Partner tries to steal the ball. 5. Player who ends up with the ball after one minute gets a point.	• Shielding • Defending • Changing direction • Field awareness	10
Activity 2 1 player vs. 1 player	1. Divide players into groups of four. 2. Two players 20 yards apart are goal posts; two players in middle play 1 player vs. 1 player. 3. Player scores by hitting the "goal post" with the ball or dribbling past the "goal post." 4. Play one minute and rotate: Goal posts become players; players become goal posts. 5. Rotate players to other groups.	• Transition • Attacking • Defending • Goal-scoring • Shielding • Tackling • Having FUN playing the game	10

Activity 3
Dribbling relay races

1. Set up two lines, each with four cones, with 20 yards between lines.

2. Assign players to four equal teams. Each team lines up behind a cone in the "home" line.

3. First player in each line dribbles around far cone in "away" line and back to "home" and gives ball to next player in line.

4. First team to have all players dribble from home to away and back to home wins.

5. Progression: dribbling with one foot, two feet, inside of feet, outside of feet, soles of feet.

- Dribbling
- Running with ball
- Field awareness

10

Activity 4
Capture all soccer balls

1. Assign players to four equal teams.

2. Each team begins in a home base in a corner of a grid.

3. Place all balls in center of grid.

4. On coach's command, each player runs to a ball and tries to return the ball to the home base by dribbling or passing the ball.

5. Players can steal balls from other teams' home bases.

6. Team with most balls at home base after one minute wins.

- Passing
- Dribbling
- Making decisions
- Defending
- Field awareness

10

Play the game:
4 players vs. 4 players

1. Set up field with goals about 30 yards apart.

2. Play 4 players vs. 4 players.

3. No limitations.

4. No goalkeepers.

- Making decisions
- Solving problems
- Dribbling
- Passing
- Having FUN playing the game
- Teamwork
- Scoring goals

15-20

Lesson plans for U-8 players - Lesson plan No. 5

Exercises	Description	Activity focus	Minutes
Activity 1 Warmup: Goal-scoring partners	1. Set up multiple goals, each goal consisting of two cones 2 yards apart, in an area 25x25 yards. 2. Pair off, one ball per pair. 3. Score as many goals as possible by passing ball through goal to partner. 4. Keep track of how many goals are scored. 5. Repeat and try to score more goals than in last attempt. 6. Progression: left foot only, right foot only, inside of foot only, etc. 25 Yards / 25 Yards	• Scoring goals • Changing directions • Passing with partner • Decision-making • Teamwork	10
Activity 2 Hitting all players	1. Set up square 25x25 yards. 2. All players move around square; two players with soccer balls try to hit the other players below knees with the balls. 3. Once hit, that player gets a ball. 4. Game ends when everyone has a ball. 	• Dribbling • Passing • Making decisions • Field awareness	10

Activity 3

2 players vs. 2 players with four goals

25 Yards

25 Yards

1. Set up grid 20x25 yards.

2. Make goals with two cones 2 yards apart in each corner of the grid.

3. Play 2 players vs. 2 players.

4. Score by dribbling or passing through either of the two goals the team attacks.

- Dribbling
- Passing
- Playing under pressure from defenders
- Defending
- Making decisions
- Having FUN playing the game

10

Activity 4

Tony chest nut

1. Each player juggles ball in a progression: foot-knee-chest-knee-head-catch with hands.

- Eye and body coordination
- Feeling comfortable with the ball

10

Play the game:

2 players vs. 2 players tournament

25 Yards

25 Yards

1. Set up square 25x25 yards with goals 12 feet wide at each end.

2. Play 2 players vs. 2 players.

3. Players score by passing through goal, dribbling through goal, or stopping ball on goal line.

4. Play 5-minute games.

5. Rotate teams so every team of two players plays every other team.

- Dribbling
- Passing
- Receiving
- Defending
- Having FUN playing the game
- Communicating
- Scoring goals

15-20

Lesson plans for U-8 players – Lesson plan No. 6

Exercises	Description	Activity focus	Minutes
Activity 1 Warmup: Dribbling relay races 	1. Set up two lines, each with four cones, with 20 yards between lines. 2. Assign players to four equal teams. Each team lines up behind a cone in the "home" line. 3. First player in each line dribbles around far cone in "away" line and back to "home," and gives ball to next player in line. 4. First team to have all players dribble from home to away and back to home wins. 5. Progression: dribbling with one foot, two feet, inside of feet, outside of feet, soles of feet.	• Dribbling • Running with ball • Field awareness	10
Activity 2 Ball racing 	1. Set up two lines 20 yards apart. 2. Divide players into two equal teams and give each player a ball. 3. Teams line up on opposite lines. 4. On coach's command, all players dribble at walking pace toward opposite lines and try to stop the ball on the lines. 5. First team that has three players stop the ball on the opposite line gets a point. 6. Progression: Players dribble while running.	• Running with ball • Changing speed • Field vision	10

Activity 3
1 player vs. 1 player

1. Divide players into groups of four.

2. Two players 20 yards apart are goal posts; two players in middle play 1 player vs. 1 player.

3. Player scores by hitting the "goal post" with the ball or dribbling past the "goal post."

4. Play one minute and rotate: Goal posts become players; players become goal posts.

5. Rotate players to other groups.

- Transition
- Attacking
- Defending
- Goal-scoring
- Shielding
- Tackling
- Having FUN playing the game

15

20 Yards

Activity 4
Shooting on goal

1. Set up a full-size goal.

2. Each player has a ball.

3. Players line up side-by-side facing goal, 6 yards away

4. On coach's command, player at one end of line shoots the ball; next player shoots immediately; continue until all players in line have shot.

5. Players retrieve balls and repeat from 12 yards, 18 yards, etc.

6. Progression: Strike with left foot, right foot, inside of foot, outside of foot, volleys, half-volleys.

- Ball striking
- Scoring goals
- Making decisions
- Keeping eye on the ball

10

6 Yards

Play the game:
4 players vs. 4 players

1. Set up field with goals about 30 yards apart.

2. Play 4 players vs. 4 players.

3. No limitations.

4. No goalkeepers.

- Making decisions
- Solving problems
- Dribbling
- Passing
- Having FUN playing the game
- Teamwork
- Scoring goals

15-20

30 Yards

20 Yards

Exercises	Description	Activity focus	Minutes
Activity 1 Warmup: Keepaway	1. Set up circle 10 or 15 yards across. 2. One player stands in the circle. 3. Remaining players stand around perimeter of circle and pass around one ball. 4. Player in middle tries to intercept a pass. 5. Rotate players into the middle every 30 seconds. 6. Progression: one touch, two touches, two players in the middle.	• Passing • Receiving • Thinking of next pass before receiving the ball • First touch	10
Activity 2 Get out of here	1. Set up square 25x25 yards with goals 12 feet wide at each end. 2. Play 2 players vs. 2 players. 3. Coach passes ball onto field to start play. 4. Game continues until a goal is scored or the ball goes out of bounds. 5. If the ball goes out of bounds, coach yells, "Get out of here," and two new teams come on field. 6. If a team scores, it stays on the field and new team comes on to resume game.	• Field awareness • Passing • Dribbling • Shooting • Defending • Getting open for a pass • Making decisions	10

10 or 15 YARDS

25 Yards

25 Yards

Activity 3
Tail tag

1. Set up square 25x25 yards.
2. Each player tucks a practice vest or shirt into the back of the shorts.
3. On coach's command, players try to take vests from other players.
4. Last player with vest tucked in wins.
5. Progression: Each player dribbles a ball while trying to take vests.

- Awareness of other players on field
- Dribbling with heads up
- Having FUN
- Shielding
- Making decisions

10

Activity 4
2 players vs. 2 players

25 Yards

25 Yards

1. Set up square 25x25 yards with goals 12 feet wide at each end.
2. Play 2 players vs. 2 players.
3. Players score by passing through goal, dribbling through goal, or stopping ball on goal line.

- Dribbling
- Passing
- Receiving
- Defending
- Having FUN playing the game
- Communicating
- Scoring goals

15-20

Play the game:
4 players vs. 4 players

20 yards

30 Yards

1. Set up field with goals about 30 yards apart.
2. Play 4 players vs. 4 players.
3. No limitations.
4. No goalkeepers.

- Making decisions
- Solving problems
- Dribbling
- Passing
- Having FUN playing the game
- Teamwork
- Scoring goals

15-20

Lesson plans for U-8 players – Lesson plan No. 8

Exercises	Description	Activity focus	Minutes
Activity 1 Warmup: Hospital tag	1. Set up square 25x25 yards. 2. Each player has a ball. 3. One player is "it." 4. When "it" tags someone, that player stops and puts hand where tagged. 5. Repeat after 30 seconds with a new player who is "it."	• Dribbling • Changing direction • Field awareness • Avoiding defender ("it")	10
Activity 2 Ball stealing	1. Set up square 25x25 yards. 2. Each player has a ball. 3. On coach's command, leave ball, steal another player's ball, and continue dribbling. 4. Progression: right foot only, left foot only, different parts of feet.	• Dribbling • Making decisions • Shielding	10

25 Yards

25 Yards

25 Yards

25 Yards

Activity 3
2 players vs. 2 players with end zones

10

1. Set up grid 12x25 yards with a 1-yard-wide end zone at each end.
2. Play 2 players vs. 2 players.
3. Teams score by dribbling and stopping ball in the end zone.
4. Defenders can't play in the end zones.

- Dribbling
- Passing
- Receiving
- Getting open for a pass
- Making decisions
- Shielding
- Defending

Activity 4
Freeze tag

10

1. Set up square 25x25 yards.
2. All players except one has a ball. Player without ball is "it."
3. Person who is "it" tags a player dribbling with a ball. That player holds ball over head, spreads legs, and is "frozen."
4. Player is "unfrozen" when a ball is dribbled between the player's legs.
5. Change person who is "it" every 45-60 seconds.

- Dribbling
- Shielding
- Peripheral vision
- Awareness of defender
- Scoring goals
- Making decisions

Play the game:
3 players vs. 3 players

15-20

1. Set up field with goals about 20 yards apart.
2. Play 3 players vs. 3 players.
3. No limitations.
4. No goalkeepers.

- Find the goal
- Dribbling past defenders
- Having FUN playing the game
- Learning which direction to run
- Scoring goals

Lesson plans for U-8 players - Lesson plan No. 9

Exercises

Activity 1
Warmup: Ball tossing

Description

1. Divide players into pairs.

2. Each player has a ball.

3. Throw or roll balls to each other.

4. Progression: Pass balls with feet.

Activity focus

· Problem solving

· Eye and body coordination

· Teamwork

· Having FUN

Minutes

10

Activity 2
Line soccer

Description

1. Set up square 25x25 yards with goals 12 feet apart at each end.

2. Divide players into teams of five players each.

3. Coach assigns each player a number from one to five.

4. One team stands on one sideline; another team stands on the opposite sideline; each team is assigned a goal to attack.

5. Ball is placed at center of field.

6. Coach calls out a number; the player with that number from each team runs on the field and those players play 1 player vs. 1 player for one minute.

7. Progression: Coach calls out two numbers; those players play 2 players vs. 2 players for one minute.

Activity focus

· Passing

· Dribbling

· Shielding

· Defending

· Teamwork

Minutes

10

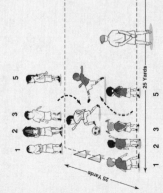

Activity 3
Marbles

1. Set up a circle 10 yards across.

2. Set up four cones, each one 15 yards from the edge of the circle.

3. Each player has a ball inside the circle.

4. Players try to kick other players' balls out of the circle.

5. When a ball is kicked out of the circle, the player has to retrieve the ball, dribble around a cone, and back into the circle.

6. Play for two minutes.

- Field awareness
- Dribbling
- Shielding
- Defending

10

Activity 4
Corner goals

1. Set up field with cones making diagonal goals in each corner.

2. Divide players into two equal teams.

3. Coach plays in a ball to start the game.

4. Goals are scored by shooting or passing the ball through any of the four goals.

5. Coach immediately plays in a new ball as soon as the ball goes out of bounds or a goal is scored.

6. Progression: Assign each team two goals to attack and two goals to defend.

- Passing
- Shooting
- Making decisions
- Defending
- Teamwork
- Field awareness
- Scoring goals

10

Play the game:
4 players vs. 4 players

1. Set up field with goals about 30 yards apart.

2. Play 4 players vs. 4 players.

3. No limitations.

4. No goalkeepers.

- Making decisions
- Solving problems
- Dribbling
- Passing
- Having FUN playing the game
- Teamwork
- Scoring goals

15-20

Lesson plans for U-8 players - Lesson plan No. 10

Exercises	Description	Activity focus	Minutes
Activity 1 Warmup: Sitting ball juggling	1. Each player sits and holds a ball over the shoelaces. 2. Kick the ball once and catch. 3. Kick the ball two times and catch. 4. Continue to five kicks and a catch. 5. Progression: right foot only; left foot only.	• Eye-feet-hands coordination • Bending knee of kicking leg • Pointing toes of kicking leg out • Driving the knee of the kicking leg to the chest when kicking the ball	10
Activity 2 Stop and go	1. Each player dribbles a ball. 2. On whistle, players stop, then go with speed. 3. Encourage players to invent own stop-and-go techniques. 4. Have players demonstrate their own stop-and-go techniques for others to copy.	• Keeping head up while dribbling • Seeing ball through bottom of eyes • Changing speeds • Changing direction	10

Activity 3
1 player vs. 2 players

15 Yards

1. Set up grids 15x15 yards.
2. Divide players into teams of threes.
3. One player dribbles; the two without the ball try to take it.
4. When a ball is taken, that player dribbles and the other two players try to take it.

• Dribbling
• Shielding
• Possessing ball under pressure

10

Activity 4
Ball tag

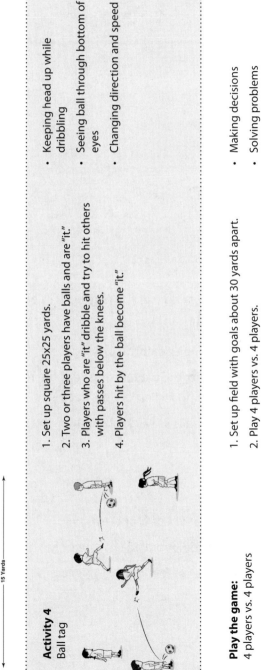

1. Set up square 25x25 yards.
2. Two or three players have balls and are "it."
3. Players who are "it" dribble and try to hit others with passes below the knees.
4. Players hit by the ball become "it."

• Keeping head up while dribbling
• Seeing ball through bottom of eyes
• Changing direction and speed

10

Play the game:
4 players vs. 4 players

30 Yards

20 Yards

1. Set up field with goals about 30 yards apart.
2. Play 4 players vs. 4 players.
3. No limitations.
4. No goalkeepers.

• Making decisions
• Solving problems
• Dribbling
• Passing
• Having FUN playing the game
• Teamwork
• Scoring goals

15-20

Exercise No. 1: Pac-Man

1. Coach stands in the middle of the playing area and is "Pac-Man."

2. Each player has a ball.

3. All players start at one end of the playing area.

4. On coach's command, the players must dribble to the far end without their soccer balls being kicked out by "Pac-Man."

5. Any players whose balls are kicked out go in the middle and become "Pac-Men."

Variations:

- Dribble using right or left foot only.
- Dribble using inside or outside of foot only.
- Dribble using soles of feet only.

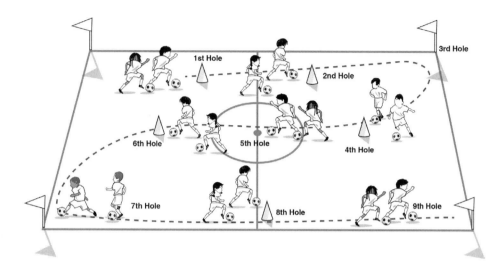

Exercise No. 2: Soccer golf

1. Each player has a ball.

2. Designate objects around the field (cones, markers, center circle, light pole, etc.) and number them as "holes."

3. Players dribble in pairs around the "golf course."

4. Each touch of the ball counts as a "stroke."

5. Each player keeps own score; lowest score wins.

Variations:

- Dribble using right or left foot only.
- Dribble using inside or outside of foot only.
- Dribble using soles of feet only.

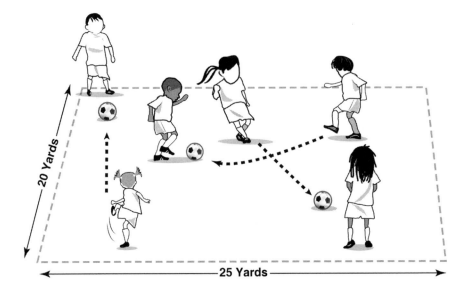

20 Yards

25 Yards

Exercise No. 3: Cover field

1.   Set up area 20x25 yards.

2.   Pair off; each pair has a ball.

3.   Coach explains that the ball is a "paint brush" and will cover the area wherever it rolls.

4.   Object is for each pair to "paint" as much of the area as possible with passes in one minute.

Variations:

  • Pass with right or left foot only.

  • Pass with inside or outside of foot only.

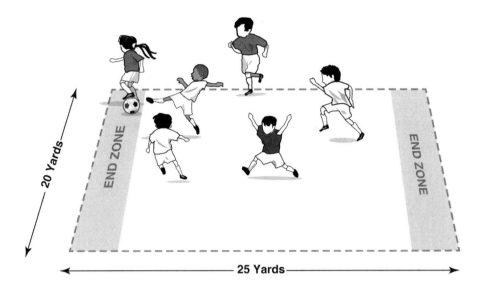

Exercise No. 4: 3v3 end zone

1. Set up area 20x25 yards with 1-yard-wide end zone at each end.

2. Play 3 players vs. 3 players.

3. Goals are scored for dribbling into and stopping the ball in the end zone.

4. Defenders can't defend in the end zones.

Variations:

- Limit to one, two or three touches.
- Enforce offsides.

Exercise No. 5: Score goals

1.   Divide players into two equal teams.

2.   Use cones to set up three goals at each end of the playing area.

3.   Goals are scored by dribbling through a goal on the opponents' end line.

4.   Defenders can't defend in the goals.

Variations:

- Limit to one, two, or three touches.
- Enforce offsides.

Exercise No. 6: Corner goals

1. Divide players into two equal teams.

2. Use cones to set up a diagonal goal in each corner of the playing area.

3. Goals are scored by passing or shooting through any of the four goals.

4. Coach plays in a new ball whenever a goal is scored or the ball goes out of bounds.

Variations:

• Assign each team two goals to attack and two goals to defend.

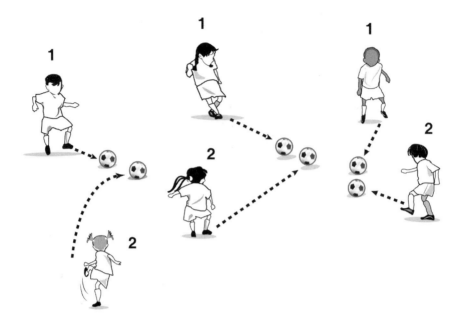

Exercise No. 7: Croquet

1. Mark out a playing area with cones.

2. Divide players into pairs, two balls per pair.

3. Player 1 plays out the ball; player 2 (the partner of player 1) tries to hit the ball with a pass for a point.

4. Each pair retrieves their balls; player 2 plays out the ball and player 1 tries to hit it with a pass for a point.

5. Continue for one minute.

6. Each pair keeps track of its points.

Variations:

- Make players try to hit each other's ball without stopping to increase the pace of the game. If player 2 misses player 1's ball, then player 1 runs to the ball and tries to hit player 2's ball with a pass. Then player 2 tries to hit player 1's ball. Continue for one minute.

Exercise No. 8: 2v1 keep-away

1. Set up a playing area 10x15 yards.

2. Play continuous 2 players vs. 1 player keep-away.

3. When the defender wins the ball, that player becomes an attacker; the attacker who lost the ball becomes the defender.

4. Balls that go out of bounds are dribbled or passed back into the grid.

5. Continue for one minute.

Variations:

  • Limit to one, two, or three touches.

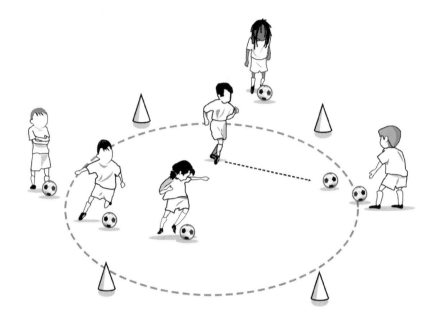

Exercise No. 9: Marbles

1. Mark out a playing area with cones.

2. Each player dribbles the ball and tries to kick other players' balls out of bounds while keeping own ball rolling.

3. A player must do two juggles to return to the game if the ball stops or is kicked out of bounds.

Exercise No. 10: Steal the ball

1. Mark out a playing area with cones.

2. Divide players into two teams.

3. Each player on one team has a ball; the other team does not have a ball.

4. Demonstrate how to shield the ball by keeping the body between the ball and a defender, using the arms, and putting the ball on the foot farthest from the defender.

5. On the coach's command, the game begins.

6. A player without the ball has to steal one from another player.

7. A ball that goes out of bounds does not belong to the player who touched it last.

U-10

Kids in the U-10 age group have reached the beginning of adolescence. Boys and girls start developing separately. They still need positive reinforcement as they did when they were U-6 and U-8 players, but they feel peer pressure as well. Their attention spans are much longer and they can stay on task. Wise coaches of U-10 players capitalize on these improved capabilities at practice and in games.

Coaches of U-10 players should:

- Include more exercises with 2v2 and 3v3 games to develop U-10 players' newly found ability to think ahead and solve more complex problems.

- Praise individual players frequently and discourage them from criticizing their teammates. But don't make phony positive comments to players who are struggling. Kids at this age are starting to recognize their own abilities.

- Provide more opportunities for players to "take charge" by giving them options, such as encouraging them to suggest an exercise or game they would like to play at the next practice.

- Tap into U-10 players' desire for more responsibility by assigning tasks. For example, put one or two players in charge of retrieving balls, picking up scrimmage vests, or collecting cones and markers at the end of practice.

These traits of U-10 players are incorporated into the following lesson plans and exercises.

Lesson plans for U-10 players - Lesson plan No. 1

Exercises	Description	Activity focus	Minutes
Activity 1 Warmup: Dribbling 	1. Use cones to set up a playing area. 2. Each player has a ball and dribbles in the playing area. 3. On coach's command, players change directions using various techniques (scissors, fake left/go right, pull back and turn, etc.). 4. Progression: Instead of using verbal commands to change directions, coach puts light pressure on players to force them to change directions.	• Using all surfaces of both feet • Keeping head up • Accelerating after changing direction • Being creative using variety of techniques to change direction	10-15
Activity 2 Hospital Tag 	1. Set up square 25 yards by 25 yards. 2. Each player has a ball. 3. One player is "it." 4. When "it" tags someone, that player stops and puts hand where tagged. 5. Repeat after 30 seconds with a new player who is "it."	• Dribbling • Changing direction • Field awareness • Avoiding defender ("it")	15

25 Yards

25 Yards

Activity 3
3 players vs. 3 players
with gates

1. Set up playing area with cones that mark out five small goals or "gates."
2. Play three players vs. three players.
3. A point is scored for dribbling through a gate or passing through a gate to a teammate.
4. Progression: Score two points if passing successfully after dribbling through a gate.

- Dribbling
- Turning
- Shielding
- Passing
- Field awareness
- Running off the ball
- Defending

15

Activity 4
Goal dribbling

1. Set up field 20 yards by 30 yards.
2. Use cones to set up a small goal at each end and two small goals on each sideline.
3. Players pair off, one ball per pair.
4. Teammates pass back and forth to each other.
5. On coach's command, player with the ball tries to dribble through one of the small goals as the teammate defends.
6. Teammate becomes the attacker after stealing the ball.
7. Continue for one minute, change teams and repeat.

- Dribbling
- Taking on a defender
- Changing directions
- Accelerating after changing directions
- Scoring
- Defending

15

30 Yards
20 Yards

Play the game:
4 players vs. 4 players

1. Set up field with goals about 30 yards apart.
2. Play 4 players versus 4 players.
3. No limitations.
4. No goalkeepers

- Making decisions
- Solving problems
- Dribbling
- Passing
- Having FUN playing the game
- Teamwork
- Scoring goals

20

30 Yards

Lesson plans for U-10 players - Lesson plan No. 2

Exercises	Description	Activity focus	Minutes
Activity 1 Warmup: Dribbling moves 	1. Set up circle 25 yards across. 2. Each player has a ball. 3. Pick a player to demonstrate a dribbling move. 4. All players do dribbling move for one minute. 5. Pick another player to demonstrate another dribbling move	• Dribbling • Using dribbling techniques (step-over, Cruyff, etc.) • Dribbling to create space • Keeping head up • Creating space	10 -15
Activity 2 Freeze tag 	1. Set up square 25 yards by 25 yards. 2. All players except one have a ball. Player without ball is "it." 3. Person who is "it" tags a player dribbling with a ball. That player holds ball over head, spreads legs and is "frozen." 4. Player is "unfrozen" when a ball is dribbled between the player's legs. 5. Change person who is "it" every 45-60 seconds.	• Dribbling • Shielding • Peripheral vision • Awareness of defender • Scoring goals • Making decisions	15

Activity 3
Goal scoring

1. Set up square 30 yards by 30 yards.
2. Use cones to make goals 2 yards wide randomly throughout the area. Have two more goals than there are pairs of players.
3. Players pair off, on ball per pair.
4. Teammates stand on either side of a goal.
5. Player throws ball through goal to partner.
6. Partner catches ball for a point and pair moves to another goal.
7. Repeat and each pair keeps track of points for 45 seconds.
8. Progression: Passing with feet; passing with right foot only; passing with left foot only; passing with inside of foot; passing with outside of foot; dribble through one gate and pass through the second.

- Scoring goals
- Striking the ball properly
- Passing
- Dribbling
- Accuracy

15

Activity 4
1 player vs. 1 player

1. Divide players into groups of four.
2. Two players 20 yards apart are goal posts; two players in middle play 1 vs. 1.
3. Player scores by hitting the "goal post" with the ball or dribbling past the "goal post."
4. Play one minute and rotate: Goal posts become players; players become goal posts.
5. Rotate players to other groups.

- Transition
- Attacking
- Defending
- Goal-scoring
- Shielding
- Tackling
- Having FUN playing the game

10

Play the game:
3 players vs. 3 players

1. Set up field with goals about 20 yards apart.
2. Play 3 players versus 3 players.
3. No limitations.
4. No goalkeepers.

- Find the goal
- Dribbling past defenders
- Having FUN playing the game
- Learning which direction to run
- Scoring goals

15-20

Lesson plans for U-10 players - Lesson plan No. 3

Exercises	Description	Activity focus	Minutes
Activity 1 Target hit 10 Yards — 20 Yards	1. Set up area 10x20 yards. 2. Place balls around outside of area. 3. One player has ball; others jog around the area. 4. Player with ball tries to pass the ball off players' knees. 5. A player hit by the ball gets a ball and also tries to pass it off other players' knees.	• Dribbling • Passing • Accuracy • Goal-scoring	10
Activity 2 Juggling 	1. Each player has a ball. 2. Juggle using feet, thigh, chest and head 3. Progression: Juggle in order of foot-foot-thigh-head. Juggle in sitting position.	• Improving eye and body coordination • Feeling comfortable with the ball • Gaining self-confidence • Creating individual goals (number of juggles)	15

Activity 3
Shooting

15

1. Set up square 25x25 yards with goals 12 feet wide at each end.
2. Play 2 players vs. 2 players, with goalkeepers. Remaining players stand in corners of square.
3. Coach serves ball from sideline to one of the players in a corner. That player begins the game, creating three players vs. two players.
4. Continue until goal is scored or ball goes out of bounds.
5. Rotate players and repeat.

- Scoring goals
- Passing
- Dribbling
- Getting open for a pass
- Defending
- Vision of field
- Communicating with teammates
- Goalkeeping

Activity 4
Freeze tag

15

1. Set up square 25 yards by 25 yards.
2. All players except one have a ball. Player without ball is "it."
3. Person who is "it" tags a player dribbling with a ball. That player holds ball over head, spreads legs and is "frozen."
4. Player is "unfrozen" when a ball is dribbled between the player's legs.
5. Change person who is "it" every 45-60 seconds.

- Dribbling
- Shielding
- Peripheral vision
- Awareness of defender
- Scoring goals
- Making decisions

Play the game:
4 players vs. 4 players

15-20

1. Set up field with goals about 30 yards apart.
2. Play 4 players versus 4 players.
3. No limitations.
4. No goalkeepers

- Making decisions
- Solving problems
- Dribbling
- Passing
- Having FUN playing the game
- Teamwork
- Scoring goals

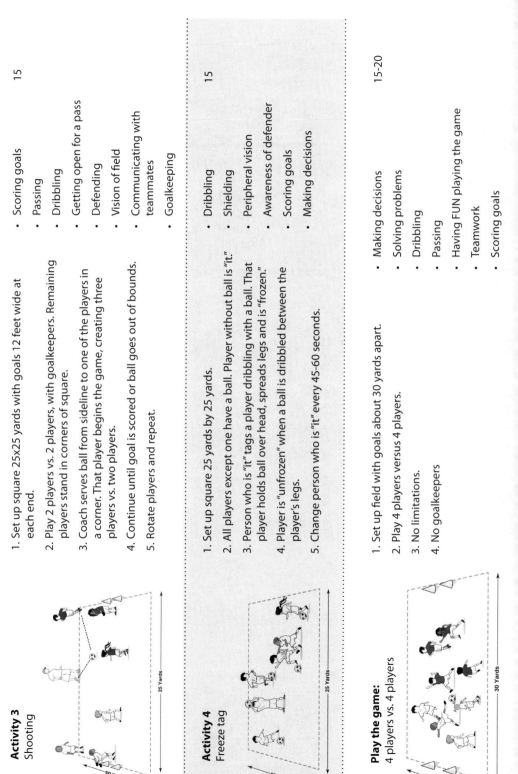

Lesson plans for U-10 players – Lesson plan No. 4

Exercises	Description	Activity focus	Minutes
Activity 1 Warmup: Dribbling to goals 	1. Players pair off, one ball per pair. 2. Use cones to set up small goals in a circle around the players. 3. Player with ball is attacker; partner is defender. 4. Attacker scores by dribbling through a goal from the inside of the circle and tries to score on a different goal by dribbling the ball through from the inside of the circle. 5. Defender becomes attacker by winning the ball.	• Dribbling • Scoring goals • Defending • Dribbling moves	10
Activity 2 World Cup 	1. Use regular goal with net. 2. Play with one goalkeeper and three teams of three players each. 3. Each team picks a country's name. 4. Coach serves in a ball from end line or sideline. 5. First team to score wins "gold medal" and leaves the field. 6. Repeat with remaining two teams; first team to score wins "silver medal." 7. Progression: Coach or player serves corner kicks.	• Goal-scoring • Defending • Teamwork • Shooting accuracy • Goalkeeping	15

Activity 3
3 players vs. 1 player

1. Three players keep the ball away from one player trying to steal the ball.
2. No designated area.
3. Go 60-90 seconds, then change person trying to steal the ball.
4. Player who steals the ball gives it back to the other three.

• Passing
• Getting open for a pass
• Receiving
• Awareness of defender

15

Activity 4
Lot of soccer balls

1. Set up area 30 yards by 40 yards. Use cones to make a goal at each end 12 feet wide.
2. Play 4 players vs. 4 players with goalkeepers.
3. Coach begins game by serving ball from sideline.
4. Coach immediately serves another ball if a goal is scored or the ball goes out of bounds.

• Scoring goals
• Passing
• Dribbling
• Getting open for a pass
• Defending
• Goalkeeping
• Having FUN playing the game (best teacher)

15

Play the game:
4 players vs. 4 players

1. Set up field with goals about 30 yards apart.
2. Play 4 players versus 4 players.
3. No limitations.
4. No goalkeepers

• Making decisions
• Solving problems
• Dribbling
• Passing
• Having FUN playing the game
• Teamwork
• Scoring goals

15-20

30 Yards

20 Yards

Lesson plans for U-10 players – Lesson plan No. 5

Exercises	Description	Activity focus	Minutes
Activity 1 Warmup: Hand ball	1. Set up area 30 yards by 40 yards. Use cones to make a small goal at each end. 2. Divide players into two equal teams. No goalkeepers. 3. Coach demonstrates various tactics. (See "activity focus.") 4. Play a "soccer" game, but players can only throw and catch the ball. No kicking. 5. Players can't steal the ball or run more than 5 feet with the ball. 6. Players score goals by getting rolling ball through goal from no farther than 3 yards away. 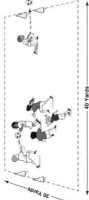	• Explaining attacking and defending roles for defenders, midfielders and forwards • Demonstrating tactics (give-and-go pass, overlap, short-short-long pass) • Easier for coach to teach and for players to learn roles and tactics using hands instead of feet.	10
Activity 2 Ball retrieve in groups	1. Set up square 50 yards by 50 yards 2. Divide players into teams of three or four, with one ball per team. 3. Coach stands in middle of square. 4. Each team starts from the edge of the square, advancing the ball to the coach through dribbling and passing. 5. Each player must touch the ball at least once before the ball reaches the coach. 6. Coach tosses the balls to the outside of the square and teams advance the ball back to the coach. 7. Progression: Advance ball using left or right foot only, or inside or outside of feet only; coach moves to different parts of the square to encourage players to look up while passing and dribbling. 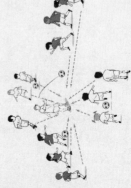	• Playing as a team • Dribbling • Passing • Receiving • Vision of field	15

Activity 3
1 player vs. 1 player

1. Divide players into groups of four.

2. Two players 20 yards apart are goal posts; two players in middle play 1 vs. 1.

3. Player scores by hitting the "goal post" with the ball or dribbling past the "goal post."

4. Play one minute and rotate: Goal posts become players; players become goal posts.

5. Rotate players to other groups.

• Transition
• Attacking
• Defending
• Goal-scoring
• Shielding
• Tackling
• Having FUN playing the game

15

20 Yards

Activity 4
Dribbling relay races

1. Set up two lines, each with four cones, with 20 yards between lines.

2. Assign players to four equal teams. Each team lines up behind a cone in the "home" line.

3. First player in each line dribbles around far cone in "away" line and back to "home" and gives ball to next player in line.

4. First team to have all players dribble from home to away and back to home wins.

5. Progression: dribbling with one foot, two feet, inside of feet, outside of feet, soles of feet.

• Dribbling
• Running with ball
• Field awareness

15

AWAY

HOME

Play the game:
4 players vs. 4 players

1. Set up field with goals about 30 yards apart.

2. Play 4 players versus 4 players.

3. No limitations.

4. No goalkeepers

• Making decisions
• Solving problems
• Dribbling
• Passing
• Having FUN playing the game
• Teamwork
• Scoring goals

15-20

30 Yards

20 Yards

Lesson plans for U-10 players - Lesson plan No. 6

Exercises

Description

Activity focus

Minutes

Activity 1
Warmup: Score goals

1. Divide players into two equal teams.
2. Place trash can in middle of area.
3. No out-of-bounds.
4. Teams score a goal by hitting the trash can with the ball.
5. Players can't be within 2 yards of the trash can.
6. Progression: Can only score on a first-time finish.

- Passing
- Receiving
- Scoring goals
- Field awareness
- Defending

10

Activity 2
Partner technique

1. Players pair off, one ball per pair.
2. Partners stand 5 yards apart.
3. Player tosses ball to partner as partner runs backward.
4. Partner must receive the ball with chest or thigh and return the ball while running backward.
5. Continue for 50 yards, then switch roles.

- Controlling ball
- Communicating
- Passing

15

Activity 3
Ole'

1. Players form circle with two players in middle.
2. Players on outside of circle keep ball from inside players.
3. Every time the ball is passed between the players in the middle, everyone says, "Ole'!"
4. Change players in middle every 45-60 seconds.
5. Transition: Limit to one or two touches.

15

- Passing
- Receiving
- First touch
- Communicating

Activity 4
1 player vs. 1 player

1. Divide players into groups of four.
2. Two players 20 yards apart are goal posts; two players in middle play 1 vs. 1.
3. Player scores by hitting the "goal post" with the ball or dribbling past the "goal post."
4. Play one minute and rotate: Goal posts become players; players become goal posts.
5. Rotate players to other groups.

15

- Transition
- Attacking
- Defending
- Goal-scoring
- Shielding
- Tackling
- Having FUN playing the game

20 Yards

Play the game:
4 players vs. 4 players

1. Set up field with goals about 30 yards apart.
2. Play 4 players versus 4 players.
3. No limitations.
4. No goalkeepers

15-20

- Making decisions
- Solving problems
- Dribbling
- Passing
- Having FUN playing the game
- Teamwork
- Scoring goals

30 Yards
20 Yards

Lesson plans for U-10 players - Lesson plan No. 7

Exercises	Description	Activity focus	Minutes
Activity 1 Dribbling moves	1. Set up circle 25 yards across. 2. Each player has a ball. 3. Pick a player to demonstrate a dribbling move. 4. All players do dribbling move for one minute. 5. Pick another player to demonstrate another dribbling move.	• Dribbling • Using dribbling techniques (step-over, Cruyff, etc.) • Dribbling to create space • Keeping head up • Creating space	10
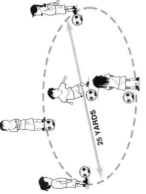			
Activity 2 Everybody is "it"	1. Set up square 25 yards by 25 yards. 2. Each player has a ball. 3. Players dribble inside area, tagging as many other players as they can. (Each player is "it.") 4. Progression: Tag person with right or left hand; tag person on shoulder; tag person on knee.	• Having FUN • Awareness of other players on field • Dribbling • Avoiding other players	15

Activity 3
3 players vs. 3 players with four goals

1. Set up playing area 20 yards by 30 yards.
2. Use cones to mark a small goal at each end and on each sideline at midfield.
3. Teams of three players defend two goals each.
4. No goalkeepers.

- Teamwork
- Scoring goals
- Changing direction
- Passing
- Field awareness
- Defending
- Learning by playing the game

15

20 Yards / 30 Yards

Activity 4
Tony chest nut

1. Each player juggles ball in a progression: foot-knee-chest-knee-head-catch with hands.

- Eye and body coordination
- Feeling comfortable with the ball

15

Play the game:
3 players vs. 3 players

1. Set up field with goals about 20 yards apart.
2. Play 3 players versus 3 players.
3. No limitations.
4. No goalkeepers.

- Find the goal
- Dribbling past defenders
- Having FUN playing the game
- Learning which direction to run
- Scoring goals

15-20

20 yards / 20 Yards

Lesson plans for U-10 players - Lesson plan No. 8

Exercises	Description	Activity focus	Minutes
Activity 1 Warmup: Passing	1. Set up square 25 yards by 25 yards. 2. Four or five players wear training vests. 3. Four or five other players dribble a ball. 4. Dribblers look for players in vests to make wall passes. 5. Progression: Players do takeovers.	• Passing • Receiving • Communicating • Field awareness	10
Activity 2 4 players vs. 4 players with four goals	1. Set up playing area 30 yards by 40 yards. 2. Use cones to mark a small goal at each end and on each sideline at midfield. 3. Teams of four players defend two goals each. 4. Score by dribbling or passing through either of the two goals the team attacks. 5. No goalkeepers.	• Teamwork • Scoring goals • Changing direction • Passing • Field awareness • Defending • Learning by playing the game	15

Activity 3
2 players vs. 2 players with four goals

1. Set up playing area 20 yards by 25 yards.
2. Make goals with two cones 2 yards apart in each corner of the grid.
3. Play 2 players vs. 2 players.
4. Score by dribbling or passing through either of the two goals the team attacks.

- Dribbling
- Passing
- Playing under pressure from defenders
- Defending
- Making decisions
- Having FUN playing the game

15

Activity 4
Freeze tag

1. Set up square 25 yards by 25 yards.
2. All players except one have a ball. Player without ball is "it."
3. Person who is "it" tags a player dribbling with a ball. That player holds ball over head, spreads legs and is "frozen."
4. Player is "unfrozen" when a ball is dribbled between the player's legs.
5. Change person who is "it" every 45-60 seconds.

- Dribbling
- Shielding
- Peripheral vision
- Awareness of defender
- Scoring goals
- Making decisions

15

Play the game:
4 players vs. 4 players

1. Set up field with goals about 30 yards apart.
2. Play 4 players versus 4 players.
3. No limitations.
4. No goalkeepers.

- Making decisions
- Solving problems
- Dribbling
- Passing
- Having FUN playing the game
- Teamwork
- Scoring goals

15-20

Lesson plans for U-10 players - Lesson plan No. 9

Exercises	Description	Activity focus	Minutes
Activity 1 Warmup: Dribbling moves 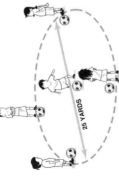 25 YARDS	1. Set up circle 25 yards across. 2. Each player has a ball. 3. Pick a player to demonstrate a dribbling move. 4. All players do dribbling move for one minute. 5. Pick another player to demonstrate another dribbling move.	• Dribbling • Using dribbling techniques (step-over, Cruyff, etc.) • Dribbling to create space • Keeping head up • Creating space	10
Activity 2 Juggling	1. Each player has a ball. 2. Juggle using feet, thigh, chest and head. 3. Progression: Juggle in order of foot-foot-thigh-head. Juggle in sitting position.	• Improving eye and body coordination • Feeling comfortable with the ball • Gaining self-confidence • Creating individual goals (number of juggles)	15

Activity 3
1 player vs. 1 player

1. Divide players into groups of four.

2. Two players 20 yards apart are goal posts; two players in middle play 1 vs. 1.

3. Player scores by hitting the "goal post" with the ball or dribbling past the "goal post."

4. Play one minute and rotate: Goal posts become players; players become goal posts.

5. Rotate players to other groups.

- Transition
- Attacking
- Defending
- Goal-scoring
- Shielding
- Tackling
- Having FUN playing the game

15

20 Yards

Activity 4
Freeze tag

1. Set up square 25 yards by 25 yards.

2. All players except one have a ball. Player without ball is "it."

3. Person who is "it" tags a player dribbling with a ball. That player holds ball over head, spreads legs and is "frozen."

4. Player is "unfrozen" when a ball is dribbled between the player's legs.

5. Change person who is "it" every 45-60 seconds.

- Dribbling
- Shielding
- Peripheral vision
- Awareness of defender
- Scoring goals
- Making decisions

15

25 Yards

25 Yards

Play the game:
4 players vs. 4 players

1. Set up field with goals about 30 yards apart.

2. Play 4 players versus 4 players.

3. No limitations.

4. No goalkeepers

- Making decisions
- Solving problems
- Dribbling
- Passing
- Having FUN playing the game
- Teamwork
- Scoring goals

15-20

30 Yards

20 Yards

Lesson plans for U-10 players - Lesson plan No. 10

Exercises	Description	Activity focus	Minutes
Activity 1 Warmup: Olé	1. Players form circle with two players in middle. 2. Players on outside of circle keep ball from inside players. 3. Every time the ball is passed between the players in the middle, everyone says, "Ole!" 4. Change players in middle every 45-60 seconds. 5. Transition: Limit to one or two touches.	• Passing • Receiving • First touch • Communicating	10
Activity 2 3 players vs. 1 player	1. Three players keep the ball away from one player trying to steal the ball. 2. No designated area. 3. Go 60-90 seconds, then change person trying to steal the ball. 4. Player who steals the ball gives it back to the other three.	• Passing • Getting open for a pass • Receiving • Awareness of defender	15

Activity 3
Everybody is "it"

1. Set up square 25 yards by 25 yards.
2. Each player has a ball.
3. Players dribble inside area, tagging as many other players as they can. (Each player is "it.")
4. Progression: Tag person with right or left hand; tag person on shoulder; tag person on knee.

• Having FUN
• Awareness of other players on field
• Dribbling
• Avoiding other players

15

Activity 4
Juggling

1. Each player has a ball.
2. Juggle using feet, thigh, chest and head
3. Progression: Juggle in order of foot-foot-thigh-head. Juggle in sitting position.

• Improving eye and body coordination
• Feeling comfortable with the ball
• Gaining self-confidence
• Creating individual goals (number of juggles)

15

Play the game:
4 players vs. 4 players

1. Set up field with goals about 30 yards apart.
2. Play 4 players versus 4 players.
3. No limitations.
4. No goalkeepers.

• Making decisions
• Solving problems
• Dribbling
• Passing
• Having FUN playing the game
• Teamwork
• Scoring goals

15-20

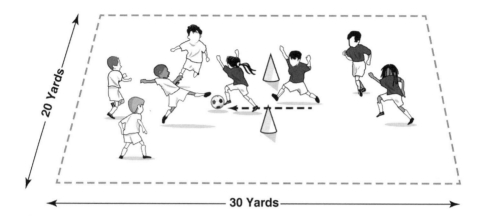

Exercise No. 1: Score from both sides

1. Set up area 20x30 yards.

2. Use cones to mark small goal in the middle of the area.

3. Play 4 players vs. 4 players.

4. Goals are scored by passing through cones from either side.

5. Defenders can't stand within 2 yards of goal.

Variations:

- Limit to one or two touches.

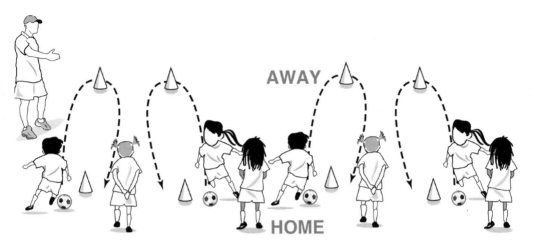

Exercise No. 2: Relay races

1. Set up two lines, each with four cones, with 20 yards between lines.

2. Assign players to four equal teams. Each team lines up behind a cone in the "home" line.

3. First player in each line runs around far cone in "away" line and back to "home;" next player in line repeats.

4. First team to have all players run from home to away and back to home wins.

Variations:

- Dribble ball around away line and back to home.
- Dribble using right or left foot only.

Exercise No. 3: Groups of 3 technique

1. Divide players into teams of three.

2. Players one and two have a ball; player three does not.

3. Player 1 throws ball to player 3, who volleys ball back to player 1.

4. Player 2 immediately throws ball to player 3, who volleys ball back to player 2.

5. Go for 60 seconds and switch roles.

6. Focus on trapping the ball with chest or thigh and then volleying with inside of foot or instep.

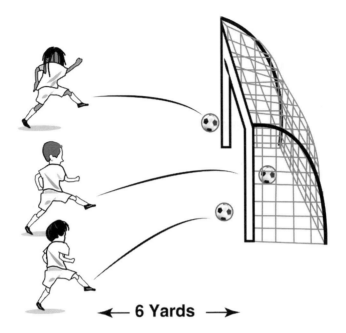

← **6 Yards** →

Exercise No. 4: Shooting

1. Each player has a ball.

2. Position players next to each other facing a regulation-size goal 6 yards away.

3. On coach's command, first player shoots, followed immediately by second player, then third player, etc., until all players have shot.

4. Players retrieve balls.

5. Repeat three times.

6. Move back to 10, then 15, then 20 yards, with players shooting four times from each distance.

Variations:

- Use instep only.

- Use inside of foot only.

- Use outside of foot only.

<u>Exercise No. 5:</u> **One bounce juggling**

1. Each player has a ball.

2. Player bounces ball and juggles using feet and thighs.

3. Player counts number of juggles before ball hits the ground.

4. Player tries to beat personal record.

Variations:

- Use right foot only, left foot only, or alternate feet.

Exercise No. 6: **Head and catch**

1. Players pair off.

2. Each pair has a ball.

3. Player tosses underhand to partner and tells partner to head or catch the ball.

4. Switch roles after 45 seconds.

Variations:

- Player does opposite of the partner's verbal command. (If told to head, player catches; if told to catch, player heads.)

Exercise No. 7: Follow your partner

1. Players pair off.

2. Each player has a ball.

3. One player leads and does whatever the player wants with the ball; partner has to follow and copy the other player's moves.

4. Go for 60 seconds, rest 30 seconds, then switch roles and repeat.

Exercise No. 8: Resting

1. Each player has a ball.

2. Coach says, "Everybody rest."

3. Players rest by touching ball with soles, inside or outside of feet, under other foot, etc., to rest and prepare for next exercise.

4. Go for 60 seconds.

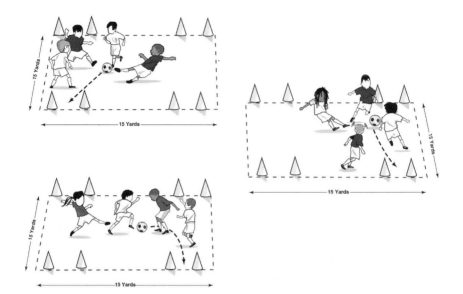

Exercise No. 9: 2 players vs. 2 players to 4 small goals

1. Set up a square 15x15 yards.

2. Use cones to set up a small goal in each corner.

3. Players pair off.

4. Play 2 players vs. 2 players.

5. Set up enough squares to have all the teams playing games at the same time.

6. Each team defends two goals and attacks the other two.

7. Ball that goes out of bounds is passed or dribbled back into square.

8. Rotate teams every 3 minutes until all teams have played each other.

Variations:

- Enlarge playing areas to 20x25 yards and play 3 players vs. 3 players.

Exercise No. 10: Circle passing

1. Use cones to set up circle 10-15 yards across.

2. Players are positioned around edge of circle.

3. One player has the ball, passes to another player, follows pass and replaces player receiving the pass.

4. Receiving player has two touches to receive and pass to another player, then follows pass and replaces player who received the pass.

5. Repeat for one minute, rest 30 seconds, and start again.

Variations:

- Unlimited touches
- One touch

Soccer Injuries:
Care and Prevention

Injuries happen. A coach must be prepared to deal with them. Most are minor cuts, bumps and bruises that are easy to treat. No matter what the injury, young players need to know that you, the coach, are concerned and will take care of them. Showing that concern goes a long way to making injured kids feel better.

There are some other general guidelines for the coach regarding injuries:

- Stay calm.
- Use common sense.
- Have a first-aid kit at all practices and games. The kit should include Band-Aids, gauze pads, antiseptic spray, elastic wrap, tape, small plastic bags for ice, rubber gloves and hand towels or wash cloths.
- Seek professional help, if possible. Medical personnel are usually on hand during league matches and tournaments.
- Check for bleeding, shock, possible broken bones and consciousness.
- Talk to the player. Ask what happened, how it happened, and where it hurts.
- Don't move the player if the injury is serious.
- Talk to the injured player's parents if they are on hand; if not, contact them afterward as soon as possible. Describe how the injury happened and how it was treated.
- If a player has medical attention for the injury, it is recommended that they have written permission from a doctor to return to practice and games.
- Take a first-aid course.

Role Models for Life

Kids are great at mimicking others. They pick up on the language, habits and attitudes displayed by people around them . . . people such as parents, teachers and coaches. If you argue with referees, belittle other coaches, and criticize poor play, don't be surprised if your U-6 or U-8 or U-10 players follow your lead. They watch everything you do. For better or for worse, you are their role model.

Here are some tips on being a good role model as a coach and as a parent.

Coaches

- Take a course on the Laws of the Game.
- Accept referees' decisions.
- Stay calm.
- Don't make loud, offensive remarks.
- Focus on coaching rather than on the accuracy of the referees' decisions.
- Support fair play at all times.
- Be positive and avoid confrontations with officials.
- Leave decisions to the players during games.
- Attend coaching classes to further your knowledge of the game.
- Give good guidelines to parents.
- Set high standards.
- Be firm with parents at games.

- Teach skills and fair tactics.
- Discourage unfair gamesmanship.
- Communicate often with parents in meetings and at social gatherings.
- Play the game; referee games; and encourage parents to do the same.
- Delegate responsibilities.

Parents

- Be knowledgeable of the game.
- Encourage fair play.
- Be supportive. Be sure your kids attend practices. Take them and pick them up on time.
- Attend games.
- Be positive or be quiet at games.
- Be respectful and expect your children to be respectful.
- Focus on good nutrition.
- Volunteer to help the coach.
- Become a referee.
- Play the game of soccer.
- Be calm and have good manners.
- Support the coach's and the referee's decisions.
- Encourage communication between you and the coach.
- Ask your children to describe their roles as players and what new skills they have learned.
- Watch practices; focus on new skills and tactics that are taught.
- Watch soccer on TV with your children.
- Praise other people's children during games.
- Read media reports about successful older players; pick out things you admire about those players; and use those things as models for your children.

Conclusion:
A Three-Letter Word Defines a Great Kids Coach

Twenty million U.S. kids sign up every year for competitive athletics, according to the National Alliance for Sports. By age thirteen, the organization reports, 70 percent of them—that's 14.1 million kids—have quit and will never play again.

Why? "The number one reason is that it stopped being fun," says Michael Pfahl, former executive director of the National Youth Sports Coaches Association.

As we've tried to show in this book, making soccer fun is the most important thing a coach can do when teaching the game to kids in the U-6, U-8, and U-10 age groups. These are the ages when kids soak up knowledge like sponges—provided that they are motivated to do so.

Fun is that motivator.

Very few youth coaches will develop players who become professionals. All youth coaches will turn out players who grow up. Years from now, when your former players are coping with the challenges of being an adult, you can bet that they won't recall the scores of any of the soccer games they played as 6-year-olds. But if they look back on those games, smile, and remember how much fun it was, you know what that says about you?

You were a great coach.